Presented to:

FURTHER
FASTER

Also by Ted Shuttlesworth Jr.

*Unhang Your Harp: How Praise Opens the Door to
Every Blessing God Has Provided for You*

Blood on the Door: The Protective Power of Covenant

Blood on the Door: Workbook

*Praise. Laugh. Repeat.: Living in the Power
of Overwhelming Joy*

*Praise. Laugh. Repeat. Devotional:
A 40-Day Journey to Overwhelming Joy*

(Also available on Apple Books and Amazon Kindle)

FURTHER FASTER

HOW TO ACCELERATE YOUR PURPOSE THROUGH THE FORCE OF IMPARTATION

TED SHUTTLESWORTH JR.

MIRACLE WORD
PUBLISHING

Published in Virginia Beach, Virginia by Miracle Word Publishing.

Miracle Word titles may be purchased in bulk for educational, business, fund-raising, or sales promotional use. For information, please e-mail info@miracleword.com

ISBN 978-0-9909196-8-1

For Madelyn, Brooklyn, and Teddy III.
May you ever exceed me.

CONTENTS

FOREWORD

One of my first memories as a child is riding on the shoulders of my father. Every kid delights in this place of height and prestige. To a toddler, the safety, security, and affection that is fostered in this age-old position is like very few other things on earth. This same feeling has warmed my heart time and time again as both a young man and now seasoned minister. The feeling of being in a place I know is beyond my ability to manufacture or maintain. It has happened to me consistently throughout my life.

Coming from a family of ministers on both sides (four on my dad's side and three on my mom's), I know what it's like to get a head start in ministry. I've directly reaped the benefits of standing on the shoulders of giants in faith and picked up where they wrapped up their race.

One distinct memory was at 19 years old. I started

receiving a salary to preach the gospel and began realizing the cost that was paid for me to enjoy such a privilege at an early age.

My grandfather, Roy Stockstill, and his dear wife Ruth, both sacrificed greatly so that I would have the privilege of starting where many simply dreamed of ending up. "Bro Roy," as he was known, would catch a ride early to the local petroleum plant where he would serve as a pipe fitter's helper in the Louisiana heat.

At lunch, he would pull out his suit, change under a nearby bridge, and go to the hospital to visit some ailing member of his newly-founded church. After making his visit, he would then return to work, put on his work clothes, and finish out the grueling workday.

My dear grandmother raised a family, taught school, and sold World Book Encyclopedias door to door in order to make ends meet while the foundling church was in its early days.

These were sacrifices I did not have to make. My godly grandparents opened doors of favor and opportunity for me. This is starting the game with a lead!

This idea of starting with a lead or standing on the shoulders of those before you is not a new concept, nor is something that only the lucky or elite can enjoy. This is a spiritual concept that is as old as time. The great news today is that regardless of your family of origin and their status economically or socially, you have been born again into a new family. This family is not flesh and blood, but something far greater — this is the family of God!

You don't need to come from four generations of preachers to start your calling and live out your purpose with a head start. You simply need to understand one word that is probably the word that drew you to this book . . . IMPARTATION!

In a day when many American families will see their kids struggle financially more than they did (for the first time in our history), the Kingdom of God is never subject to these natural limitations. You should never feel as if you have to "start from scratch" in your pursuit of God's call on your life. You have a divine destiny, and there is an impartation waiting for you!

With 2000 years of church history, generations of men and women of God giving their lives, days spent in prayer, hours spent in study, decades spent honing doctrine, centuries spent contending for the full gospel, there is NO REASON for you ever to believe the lie that you can't start your journey with the collective force of all God has done in ages past. It will be like a strong wind at your back!

Now we come to the real question of this book. *How do I tap into this awesome power for my life?* So glad you asked and so thankful for Ted Shuttlesworth Jr.'s insight. His family and life are a prime example of this principle in full effect.

Join him on a journey as he lights the way to tapping into everything that's available by the power of impartation. His simple, spiritual, and humorous style will help you press into this awesome power at your disposal.

I pray that by the end of this book, you will have the same warm feeling I had as a child and have enjoyed throughout my life of standing on the shoulders of giants and starting where others left off.

I pray you will catch the heart of a man who truly lives this principle every day and is actively passing on this heavenly head start to his own family.

I pray that you will be encouraged and strengthened to believe in the "head start" you have as a child of God.

I pray all feelings of fear and inferiority would be defeated. Buckle your seat belt and get ready to unleash the power of IMPARTATION!

Pastor Joel Stockstill
Executive Director, The Surge Project

CHAPTER 1

WHAT IS IMPARTATION?

For I long to see you, that I may impart to you some
spiritual gift to strengthen you.
— Romans 1:11 ESV

I ran across the patio of the lanai, leaped into the air, and landed a perfect cannonball in the shallow end of our pool effectively soaking my kids before they could ease their way into the water.

After Madelyn and Brooklyn finished their whiny protests of my dad-like harassment, they jumped into the pool with me.

We had just moved from Virginia Beach, Virginia, where Carolyn and I had lived for thirteen years, to Parkland, Florida.

When you move to a place where the average year-round temperature is 84 degrees Fahrenheit (29 degrees Celsius for those of you on the crazy metric system that Americans can never seem to understand), it's essential to develop a good cannonball. We decided that in the heat of the day, it would be better to play in the pool.

Madelyn, my oldest daughter, is extremely competitive (not sure where she gets that), and Brooklyn has a healthy dose of middle-child syndrome.

So, any time we start playing, it becomes more of a contest than anything. Who's going to win? Who will get the most of daddy's attention? Who gets to lay on the massive unicorn raft? (The answer to the last one is *me*.)

That day, the competition was a swimming race. Maddy had a clear advantage here because she's three years older and at the time of this story a much better swimmer.

Also, with her extremely competitive nature, there's no way she'd take the high road and let her younger sister win a race or two.

As a result, after a couple of races and continued frustration, Brooklyn was in tears and claiming that somehow Maddy had cheated in the race.

"Let's do one more race," I said and winked at Brooklyn when Maddy wasn't looking. Suddenly, her red eyes and little pout were transformed into a mischievous grin as she realized what daddy's wink meant.

I stood behind Brooklyn as they lined up for the final race. I began the countdown, and the girls took their ready positions.

"Three, two, one, go!" I shouted. Maddy pushed off of the wall at the shallow end and began swimming furiously toward the other side.

Now that she wasn't looking, I held Brooklyn tightly and pushed her forward with all the strength I had. I launched her past Maddy, who didn't immediately notice because she was swimming underwater.

Brooklyn's little legs kicked hard, and she splashed noisily as she battled for the win. When Maddy came up for air and noticed Brooklyn swimming ahead of her, she was baffled. She struggled to catch up, but it was no use.

Moments later, Brooklyn grabbed the wall on the other side of the pool and squealed with delight the way only four-year-old girls can do.

Maddy, realizing what had happened, turned around and peered at me through squinted eyes. "Daddy!" She scolded. But it was too late. Brooklyn had won, and I was already lounging on the massive unicorn raft.

IMPARTATION: GOD'S PROMOTION PLAN

The story of Brooklyn's swimming victory is a picture of what impartation looks like and how it functions.

The word *impartation* simply means to bestow a quality or attribute to someone or something that was not previously there.

In this case, Brooklyn didn't have the strength or skill to defeat her older sister in a swimming race. However, when I imparted strength to her by launching her forward, she was able to win a victory that was previously unwinnable. She was able to go further faster.

Her mischievous grin was a sign that she understood that her daddy was going to use his strength to help her.

IMPARTATION IS BESTOWING A QUALITY OR AN ATTRIBUTE TO SOMEONE THAT WASN'T THERE PREVIOUSLY.

Furthermore, it was a sign that she *wanted* my help to win the race.

Notice that when I held her and was preparing to push her forward, she wasn't kicking, screaming, and trying to get away from me.

As I'll show you in later chapters, it's not enough to know that impartation exists, you have to *desire* the impartation that's available to you.

Impartation doesn't happen randomly or by accident. It's always the result of a calculated effort on behalf of those seeking it and those giving it.

Whether it be Moses and Joshua, Elijah and Elisha, Jesus and his disciples, or Paul and Timothy, we see impartation taking place throughout the Bible to propagate the particular vision God delivered to each of his men.

The same is true today. There is already someone who is doing what you're called to do at a much greater level. It's your job to locate that person and, by faith and the grace of God, receive a spiritual deposit from them.

As I've said many times before, God doesn't want his children to learn by destruction; he wants us to learn by instruction. What I mean is that God doesn't want to use trial and error as a teaching aid.

God is the very source of wisdom. As the Psalmist wrote, "his understanding is infinite." (See Psalm 147:5.) God is also extremely efficient. Notice what the Apostle Paul wrote to the church under the inspiration of God's Spirit:

> *Therefore be careful how you walk, not as unwise men but as wise, making the most of your time, because the days are evil.*
>
> *Ephesians 5:15-16 NLT*

We are to become more like God. It would be foolish to think that God expects efficiency from us while he is inefficient.

I love the way the New Living Translation renders verse 16: "make the most of your time."

That means God is also actively making the most of

his time. So let's think about it logically. First, we know that God has a plan that he has tasked us with fulfilling. We call this "The Great Commission." Because of Bible prophecy, we also know that the fulfillment of God's agenda is time-sensitive. As we near the rapture of the church, there is less and less time to complete the tasks he has given us.

Secondly, God is the one who gives his children their respective gifts and callings. The Scripture teaches that we all have different gifts and callings, and we function in different administrations. (See 1 Corinthians 12:12-31.)

However, no one's gift is entirely unique. There is someone already working for God who's operating in the same gift or calling that you've been given. Many of these men and women are far more developed in their gift or calling than you are and can help you excel in what God has called you to do.

IMPARTATION NEVER HAPPENS BY ACCIDENT. IT'S THE RESULT OF A CALCULATED EFFORT ON BEHALF OF THOSE GIVING IT AND THOSE RECEIVING IT.

Using pastors as an example, more-fruitful pastors can impart to less-fruitful pastors. Notice I didn't say *older* pastors impart to *younger* pastors.

While the Bible does speak about older men and women training younger men and women in godliness (Titus 2:2-5), respecting and honoring your elders (1 Timothy 5:1-2), and submitting yourself to them and one another (1 Peter 5:5), it doesn't mean that age is an indication of spiritual development.

On the contrary, it's possible to be older in years and still be spiritually immature. This is one of the reasons that Paul encouraged Timothy, his son in the gospel, by writing these words to him:

> *Command and teach these things. Let no one despise you for your youth, but set the believers an example in speech, in conduct, in love, in faith, in purity.*
> *1 Timothy 4:11-12 ESV*

Paul instructed Timothy, a younger man, to command and teach the things he'd learned from Paul to the *entire* assembly. It was clear that there would be people in the church who were older than Timothy and may have felt that he was unqualified to teach them because of his age.

Paul immediately corrected this thought process and reminded Timothy that impartation, not age, is what empowers you to make an impact in God's kingdom.

Insecurity about his age may have been an area where Timothy struggled mentally and needed further encouragement from Paul. This verse suggests that Timothy might have considered his young age to be a roadblock when ministering to God's people and caused him to have some anxiety about his gift as well.

In the Apostle Paul's second letter to Timothy, he gives him these specific instructions:

> *I remind you to fan into flame the gift of God, which is in you through the laying on of my hands, for God gave us a spirit not of fear but of power and love and self-control.*
>
> **2 Timothy 1:6-7 ESV**

Paul reminds Timothy that there's no reason to be afraid. Paul had already imparted a spiritual gift to Timothy when he laid hands on him, thereby empowering him to become productive in the body of Christ.

Although we should excel in spiritual maturity and fruitfulness as we get older, many do not.

As a result, some older ministers have more life experience but have made far less impact than those who may be younger but have received spiritual gifts through proper impartation.

I understand that this may be a controversial thought to some of you who are reading this book, but as I will show you from the Scripture in the upcoming chapters, God desires fruitfulness and increase from his workers.

Remember this: faithfulness without fruitfulness is foolishness.

POWER THAT'S PASSED ON

God's desire to work efficiently in his kingdom requires the use of impartation to ensure that the next generation can begin where the previous generation finished.

Imagine how foolish it would be to have each new generation of kingdom servants start at the ground level. By neglecting all the power, wisdom, and work of the previous generation, they'd have to relearn everything from scratch.

What a waste of time.

However, because so many have neglected impartation or are ignorant of the principles, that's what's happening to many people.

GOD WANTS HIS CHILDREN TO LEARN BY INSTRUCTION RATHER THAN DESTRUCTION.

What would happen if in each generation, the discoveries and research of every scientist was burned upon his or her death so that no other scientist could see it?

Where would we be technologically? How far would we have progressed from the Dark Ages? Just think of the advanced products we use today because of companies that have built on the research and development of previous generations.

For example, Apple may have developed the iPhone, but they didn't invent microchips, cellular networks, touchscreens, or the ability to mine, refine, and shape aluminum and glass. A product that took a generation by storm is the result of thousands of years of technological and scientific development. Apple built on the shoulders of giants. That's the power of impartation at work.

In the same way, God doesn't want you to have to learn from scratch. He has placed men and women on the earth to impart knowledge, revelation, power, and virtue to every generation.

> *Now these are the gifts Christ gave to the church: the apostles, the prophets, the evangelists, and the pastors and teachers. Their responsibility is to equip God's people to do his work and build up the church, the body of Christ.*
> *Ephesians 4:11-12 NLT*

Notice that although Saul, who later became the Apostle Paul, didn't initially believe Christ was the

Messiah, he learned that truth firsthand from the Lord himself (See Acts 9:3-6).

Later, as Paul was ministering for the Lord in Ephesus, the men he met didn't have to wait for an individual encounter with the Lord to learn this same truth. They were able to receive an impartation of knowledge and revelation directly from Paul. When Paul arrived in Ephesus and met these men, he asked them:

> *"Did you receive the Holy Spirit when you believed?" He asked them. "No," they replied, "we haven't even heard that there is a Holy Spirit."*
>
> *Acts 19:2 NLT*

After he taught them, he imparted the power of the Holy Spirit to these twelve men, and they began to speak in tongues and prophesy. (See Acts 19:5-6.)

Paul possessed something supernatural that they needed and was able to deliver it to them effortlessly.

When this impartation took place, they were filled with power, authority, the ability to be guided by God's voice, and much more.

These men couldn't have naturally produced what Paul gave them supernaturally. Essentially, Paul did for them spiritually what I did for my daughter physically.

That's what impartation is. It's a supernatural force that pushes you forward with divine momentum empowering you to accomplish God's purpose in an expedited manner.

As you read this book, I pray that God opens your eyes to his process of divine impartation and gives you a hunger to increase within your gifts and purpose.

As you see how God has used this process since the beginning of time to gain victory after victory for his people, may you obtain a new vision of what's possible in your life and ministry.

What does God have in store for you that will launch you forward into the most impactful days you've ever seen? Let's find out.

CHAPTER 2

YOU CANNOT HAVE WHAT YOU CANNOT SEE

*"You have asked a hard thing; yet, if you see me as I
am being taken from you, it shall be so for you . . ."*
— 2 Kings 2:10 ESV

Prophetic vision caused a lot of problems for God's enemies throughout the Bible. It was a divine advantage that often thwarted their evil plans.

One memorable example took place during a time when the King of Syria was at war with Israel. Every time he created battle plans and mobilized his forces, God would reveal the plans to Elisha, the prophet. Elisha would then warn the King of Israel, and the attack against them would fail.

After this happened several times, the King of Syria became furious and understandably paranoid. He called his officers together for a meeting.

"Which of you is the traitor? Who has been informing the King of Israel of my plans?" He demanded.

"It's not us, my lord the king," one of the officers replied. "Elisha, the prophet in Israel, tells the king of Israel even the words you speak in the privacy of your bedroom!"

"Go and find out where he is," the king commanded, "so I can send troops to seize him." (2 Kings 6:11-13.)

Once they discovered that Elisha was staying in Dothan, the King of Syria sent a great army with many chariots and horses to surround the city in the night.

The next morning, when Elisha's servant went outside and saw the troops, horses, and chariots, he immediately began to panic. He lost his peace.

Elisha, however, was as calm as ever. Nothing in the Scripture suggests Elisha ever had to get past fear to trust the Lord and walk by faith.

WHAT YOU CAN SEE IN THE SPIRIT DETERMINES WHAT YOU CAN HAVE.

"Don't be afraid!" Elisha told him. "For there are more on our side than on theirs!"

Then Elisha prayed a simple prayer: "Oh Lord, open his eyes and let him see!" When his servant looked up, he saw that horses and chariots of fire filled the hillside around their enemies.

Elisha had access to supernatural peace that his servant didn't have. Why was this?

He could see what his servant couldn't see.

Divine revelation was an advantage that allowed him to benefit from something that his servant initially could not. Revelation is vitally important because it's the master key that will enable you to access freedom that has already been provided by God.

OPEN EYES = OPEN DOORS

Not only is this concept presented to us through Old Testament stories, but it's also a principle that's taught to New Testament believers.

When Jesus was addressing people who believed that he was the Messiah, he indicated that it was their faithfulness to his teaching that defined them as disciples.

Furthermore, he told them that their freedom was dependent upon the divine truth hidden in his life-giving words.

> ***And you will know the truth, and the truth will set you free.***
> *John 8:32 NLT*

Jesus was clear that his words were not ordinary. He taught us that his words were spiritual life as they came out of his mouth (John 6:63).

There's a reason for this. Everything Jesus said came

directly from the mouth of the Father in Heaven (John 12:49). Jesus was a pipeline to the throne room of God.

That's why, even in seemingly impossible situations, he could boldly proclaim:

> *. . . All things are possible for one who believes.*
>
> **Mark 9:23 ESV**

For one who believes what? His mighty word.

The devil works in the darkness. Scripture teaches that there are men who love the darkness because their deeds are evil (John 3:19).

The devil can *only* work in the darkness. That's why he wants to keep you in the dark. Notice what happens when God's Word comes:

> *The entrance of Your words gives light; it gives understanding to the simple.*
>
> **Psalm 119:130 NKJV**

When God's Word comes, it brings light. It's a light that cannot be extinguished and cannot be overpowered. This is why the truth—God's holy Word—is the catalyst that activates your freedom.

Let's look at a dynamic description of God's Word:

*And the Light shines on in the darkness,
for the darkness has never overpowered
it [put it out or absorbed it or appropri-
ated it, and is unreceptive to it].*

John 1:5 AMP

That's a powerful verse. Darkness has never (and will never) overpower the light of God's Word. It would not matter if all of hell aligned itself against one word spoken by God. There is more power in that one word than is contained in all the forces of hell.

Even death — which the Apostle Paul called the final enemy — didn't have enough darkness to overpower the light of God's Word.

When Jesus stood in front of Lazarus' tomb, he simply spoke three words: *"Lazarus, come forth."* When he did, a man who had been dead and decomposing for four days immediately came back to life.

Three words of life overpowered four days of death.

Three words of light overcame four days of darkness. Nothing compares to the unstoppable light of God's Word.

What you can *see* in God's Word determines the freedom you can experience. Paul not only understood this concept, he considered it to be so important that he made it his prayer for the churches.

EMPOWERMENT BY ENLIGHTENMENT

Paul dealt differently with all the churches because they were at varying levels of maturity. The Corinthians in Greece were babies and extremely immature. Paul was frustrated having to continually feed them milk (1 Corinthians 3:1-2).

The Ephesians, on the other hand, were on a much higher level. They were possibly the most mature church in the New Testament.

In his letter to the Ephesians, Paul prayed potent and specific prayers:

> *The Father of glory, may give to you the spirit of wisdom and revelation in the knowledge of Him, the eyes of your understanding being enlightened; that you may know . . . what are the riches of the glory of His inheritance in the saints, and what is the exceeding greatness of His power . . .*
>
> *Ephesians 1:17-19 NKJV*

In these three verses, we can see the culmination of the revelation principle.

Paul asks God to give the believers a spirit of wisdom

and revelation and prays that the eyes of their understanding would be enlightened. His prayer reveals that not every believer possesses the same level of revelation of God's Word.

There are quite a few believers who are uncomfortable with the thought process that there are varying levels of realized blessing and advancement within God's kingdom.

For example, many believers in certain denominations hold the belief that viewing the baptism in the Holy Spirit as a subsequent experience to salvation is harmful because it creates a perceived "caste system" within the body of Christ.

Meaning that if you claim to receive benefits that came as a result of an experience outside of salvation, that somehow you're claiming that salvation is not enough or that believers who don't receive those benefits aren't spiritual enough.

The problem with this argument is that there are clear examples of varying development and ability in the New Testament. Paul specifically rebukes some believers for being fleshly rather than spiritual.

The reason I'm drawing your attention to this point is that some may think having a revelation of God's Word is unnecessary.

This is a dangerous way of thinking because it excludes you from the benefits that Paul taught accompany the revelation and enlightenment that come from God.

Revelation allows you to take part in the glorious riches of God's inheritance as well as the exceeding greatness of his power.

YOU WILL SUFFER THE CONSEQUENCES OF THE REVELATION YOU REJECT

Everything we receive from God is received by faith. But our faith must be founded on what is *actually* taught in Scripture. Notice how faith comes to you:

> *So then faith comes by hearing, and hearing by the word of God.*
> *Romans 10:17 NKJV*

Because of this principle, faith is compartmentalized. Let me illustrate.

Ships and submarines built for the Navy are created with compartments separated by hatches. That way, if any part of the hull is breached, they can isolate the threat by closing the hatches on either side of the compartment that has sustained damage.

Now, instead of water flooding the entire ship or submarine, it's contained to one compartment. In the same way, your salvation covenant is also compartmentalized. Although Christ purchased many wonderful spiritual blessings with which to flood your life (Ephesians 1:3), if you don't have a revelation of them, they are unattainable. The hatch is closed to you.

IGNORANCE ISN'T BLISS

The first way this happens is when people are unaware of what's available to them.

When the Apostle Paul traveled to Ephesus in Acts chapter 19, he encountered twelve men who were disciples.

"Did you receive the Holy Spirit when you believed?" He asked them.

"No," they replied, "we haven't even heard that there is a Holy Spirit."

He then asked them which baptism they had received. They revealed that it was John's baptism (in water). These men in Ephesus hadn't received the news about the available salvation that had come through Jesus' death and resurrection.

Paul revealed what Christ had done, and they became Christians. Directly afterward, he laid hands on them, and they were filled with the Holy Spirit and spoke in tongues. (See Acts 19:1-7.)

In this first example, it was impossible for these men to have faith in Christ for salvation or faith to receive the Holy Spirit because they had never heard of either one.

> IGNORANCE OF YOUR COVENANT BLESSINGS IS ENOUGH TO KEEP THEM OUT OF YOUR LIFE.

This is literally what Paul was teaching in Romans 10:17. If you study the whole chapter, he's making the point that people cannot be saved unless someone preaches the gospel to them and gives them something in which to believe (Romans 10:13-15).

Sadly, modern-day Christians can find themselves in this state because there are leaders who will not preach the *whole counsel of God* (Acts 20:16-17).

For example, it's impossible to have faith to receive healing if no one has ever told you Jesus still heals, it's his will for you to be healed, and he took stripes upon his back for your healing (1 Peter 2:24).

As a result, you can have faith to be saved because someone preached the gospel to you, but have no faith to be healed because those facts have been hidden from you.

So faith is not an all-encompassing force that overpowers what you don't know. It's a spiritual substance that is subject-specific.

The light of God's Word has to enter each part of your life if you want to be free in every area.

DAMNED IF YOU DOUBT

The second way this happens is when someone hears God's Word and rejects it as truth. This is doubt or unbelief. Believe it or not, doubt and unbelief even occurred during the ministry of Jesus.

When he traveled back to his hometown to minister, the gospel of Mark says:

> *He could do no mighty work there, except that he laid his hands on a few sick people and healed them. And he marveled because of their unbelief . . .*
>
> *Mark 6:5-6 ESV*

Even as the Son of God, Jesus' power could not override their unbelief. They rejected the truth that he was the Messiah and, as a result, couldn't benefit from his supernatural abilities.

You will suffer the consequences of the revelation you reject. There were plenty of sick people in his hometown, but they continued to suffer because they rejected the truth.

If you're a part of a church that teaches specific blessings Jesus died for aren't for today (e.g. healing, the baptism in the Holy Spirit, etc.), they're depositing doubt and unbelief into your heart.

Although all spiritual leaders will answer to God for what they teach and preach, in the meantime, you'll suffer from a lack of truth that could set you free.

It's mind-blowing that Thomas, who was a handpicked disciple of Christ, had so much doubt and unbelief in his heart that he couldn't even receive the news of Jesus' resurrection with joy.

Instead of walking by faith and not by sight, he decided he would walk by sight and not by faith. It's dangerous to hear the truth of God's Word and reject its application because it renders you helpless when the devil attacks your life.

IMPARTATION REQUIRES FAITH

I began this chapter by explaining the importance of having revelation of God's Word by faith. Although impartation is God's established system to advance his agenda, it cannot properly function if you don't believe it exists.

God is not pleased in the absence of faith (Hebrews 11:6). The shocking truth taught in Scripture is that anything that is not from faith is *sin* (Romans 14:23).

That verse shows us just how much God values a life marked by actions of faith.

As I showed you in Mark chapter 6, a lack of faith stopped people from receiving an impartation of miracle-working power.

This is one of the reasons I felt the urgency to write this book for a new generation of believers. While the enemy would love to slow the progress of God's plan on the earth by eliminating the principles of impartation, we can't let go of the promises and plans of God, which empower us to succeed.

More than ever, we need impartation. It's not only vital that we believe impartation exists, but we must also believe that it's available to us.

If we think impartation happens randomly or by the sovereign choice of God, we'll never pursue it and, truthfully, would have no reason to desire it.

I'll show you in the upcoming chapters that not only is impartation real, but it's also available to you. Furthermore, I'll give you actionable steps that will allow you to receive impartation in your own life and ministry.

THE IMPARTATION OF SPIRITUAL GIFTS WILL TRANSFORM YOU FROM USELESS TO USEFUL. // #FURTHERFASTER

CHAPTER 3

CAN MEN AND WOMEN IMPART SPIRITUAL GIFTS?

*Fan into flame the gift of God, which is in you
through the laying on of my hands . . .*
— 2 Timothy 1:6 ESV

Recently, I came across an article that was published by a Pentecostal denomination. Something I read disturbed me.

Scholars wrote the article to establish the denomination's position on the subject of impartation. The context of the article was whether or not someone could impart one or all of the nine gifts of the Spirit as defined by the Apostle Paul in 1 Corinthians chapter 12.

It was the position of the denomination that only the Holy Spirit can give the gifts of the Spirit; no individual can freely give them to another.

In one sense, I agree that no one owns the gifts of the Spirit. We are filled with the Holy Spirit, who is the giver of the gifts.

However, God uses Spirit-filled believers to impart to others in the body of Christ. The Holy Spirit works with and through Christians — not independently of them.

As I was finishing the article, I came across a few sentences that grated against my heart. The author wrote:

> Only the Holy Spirit can give supernatural gifts. There is no record in Scripture of humans prophetically imparting spiritual gifts.[1]

The problem with this portion of the article is that we have records in the Old and New Testaments of people imparting spiritual gifts to other individuals.

Since we're explicitly discussing New Testament believers, however, let's begin by focusing on evidence in the New Testament.

SPIRITUAL GIFTS IN THE NEW TESTAMENT

In 1 Corinthians chapter 12, the Apostle Paul begins to teach about the Gifts of the Spirit. He cements the importance of this subject in their minds:

> *Now concerning spiritual gifts, brothers,*
> *I do not want you to be uninformed.*
> *1 Corinthians 12:1 ESV*

Here, the two words *spiritual gifts* are translated from one Greek word: *pneumatikos*, which means things of the Spirit, or spiritual things.

Paul wanted the Corinthians to understand the weight of importance that lies upon the things of the Spirit. This is because Paul knew that the demonstration of the Spirit is paramount in ministering the gospel to the world. Notice what he wrote earlier in this same letter:

> *And my speech and my preaching were not with persuasive words of human wisdom, but in demonstration of the Spirit and of power, that your faith should not be in the wisdom of men but in the power of God.*
>
> *1 Corinthians 2:4-5 NKJV*

It's possible that Paul knew that the Corinthians (who were still very young in faith) might be tempted to revert to philosophical methods when discussing and sharing Christianity.

Greece (where Corinth is located) could be considered the epicenter of philosophy at that time. Paul's debate with the Epicurean and Stoic philosophers in Athens would undoubtedly help to substantiate this claim.

(See Acts chapter 17.)

The Apostle Paul lists and categorizes the gifts of the Spirit for the first time in 1 Corinthians chapter 12. Before this, no one had fully defined them.

Before he transitions into teaching on the power of love, Paul gives a fascinating command:

> *But earnestly desire the best gifts . . .*
> *1 Corinthians 12:31 NKJV*

After explaining the importance of spiritual gifts, Paul commands believers to desire them earnestly.

It's essential to note that the Greek word translated "gift" is *charisma*. This word means a spiritual endowment.

The word *charisma* is always used in the context of a spiritual gift or endowment and is never used to describe a natural gift or a present. (Greek words such as *doron* and *didomi* describe natural gifts.)

This is an important distinction because when we define what was meant in Scripture when someone discusses the administration of a gift, we will know if they are talking about spiritual or natural gifts.

According to the article I read, we shouldn't be able to find one record of any person imparting spiritual gifts to another person in the New Testament.

Supposedly, this is something that is done independently by the Holy Spirit with no human involvement or assistance.

PAUL: A MAN OF IMPARTATION

The writings of the Apostle Paul command more real estate in the New Testament than those of any other author. The Lord powerfully used him to impact the early church. We will see that impartation played a significant role in completing the tasks God assigned to him.

First, I want you to look at how Paul interacted with Timothy. Timothy was Paul's spiritual son or protege. He received two letters from Paul that were divinely inspired by the Holy Spirit. Notice Paul's encouragement to Timothy:

> . . . *fan into flame the gift of God, which is in you through the laying on of my hands,*
>
> *2 Timothy 1:6 ESV*

Once again, the word "gift" here is *charisma*. Paul is warning Timothy not to be overtaken by a spirit of fear by reminding him that a spiritual gift was imparted into his spirit when Paul laid hands on him.

As I'll show you in another chapter, the laying on of hands is one of the ways that impartation takes place.

Although one example of believers imparting spiritual gifts to others is enough to set a precedent, I want to give you a few other instances so that you can see that this was a method that was employed to establish God's plan in the church.

Through Paul's letters, we learn that Timothy was a man who received impartation from multiple streams. Paul draws attention to the impartation Timothy received through his godly family:

> *I am reminded of your sincere faith, a faith that dwelt first in your grandmother Lois and your mother Eunice and now, I am sure, dwells in you as well.*
>
> **2 Timothy 1:5 ESV**

Timothy was a beneficiary of imparted faith. The reason we know that his faith was imparted is that faith is a spiritual substance that must be received by supernatural means.

Faith is not hereditary. That's why it's possible for parents to serve the Lord while their children do not.

As I wrote previously, although he was a young man, Timothy was in a position to be an effective minister because of the divine impartation he had received throughout his life.

GROUP IMPARTATION

Another fascinating element of impartation is the ability to transfer spiritual gifts to many people at one time. This is something that Paul had experience with as well.

When Paul wrote to the Roman church, he gave them a preview of what he wanted to take place when he arrived in Rome:

> *For I long to see you, that I may impart to you some spiritual gift to strengthen you —*
>
> *Romans 1:11 ESV*

Interestingly, one of the main reasons Paul wanted to visit the church of Rome was to deliver an impartation of some spiritual gift to the entire assembly. What would the result be? Spiritual strength.

Notice how the Holy Spirit inspired Paul to word this phrase: *that I may impart to you . . .*

The Holy Spirit was not offended at the assumption that spiritual gifts would be imparted from one Spirit-filled believer to another. Paul had developed spiritual gifts and strength that he could distribute to other believers for their benefit.

It seems that this may have been a common occurrence in the ministry of Paul. He wrote to the Corinthian church a second time with a desire very similar to what he described to the Romans:

> *. . . I wanted to come to you first, so that you might have a second experience of grace.*
>
> **2 Corinthians 1:15 ESV**

It's worth noting that the word "grace" (meaning spiritual gift) used here is the Greek word *charis* the root word of *charisma* that can be traced back several centuries before Paul's writing.[2]

Paul seemed to relay the notion to the churches he visited that he could deliver spiritual gifts to them whenever he would visit.

FROM USELESS TO USEFUL BY IMPARTATION

We've already established that the impartation of spiritual gifts can strengthen and develop a believer or entire body of believers (Romans 1:11). However, another vital aspect of receiving spiritual gifts is that it equips you to become effective within the body of Christ.

Within Paul's short letter to Philemon, we read the story of a man named Onesimus. When Onesimus was initially in the company of Philemon, he was considered to be useless.

However, through Paul's impartation, Onesimus became useful to serve effectively and indeed is described in Paul's letter to the Colossians as "faithful" and "beloved."

> *I appeal to you for my child, Onesimus, whose father I became in my imprisonment. (Formerly he was useless to you, but now he is indeed useful to you and to me.)*
>
> *Philemon 1:10-11 ESV*

What caused the transition in the life of Onesimus? Paul tells Philemon clearly in verse 10 that he became Onesimus's *father* while he was in prison.

The same thing that qualified Timothy to be effective and useful—the spiritual gift that Paul deposited in him—was the same thing that made Onesimus useful after the time he spent with Paul.

After his resurrection, Christ did the same thing when sending his disciples into ministry:

> *Jesus said to them again, "Peace be with*
> *you. As the Father has sent me, even so I*
> *am sending you." And when he had said*
> *this, he breathed on them and said to*
> *them, "Receive the Holy Spirit."*
>
> *John 20:21-22 ESV*

Immediately, his disciples received an impartation of the Holy Spirit—a gift that strengthened them to be effective in their future purpose.

This change from useless to useful is most notable in the life of Peter. The account of his life seems to be one of extremes. Peter walked on water one moment (the only disciple to do so) and denied his relationship with Christ another moment.

When Peter rebuked Jesus for prophesying about his redemptive act of crucifixion, Jesus responded, "Get behind me, Satan! You are a hindrance to me." (See Matthew 16:21-23.)

> **SPIRITUAL GIFTS DRAMATICALLY INCREASE YOUR USEFULNESS IN THE BODY OF CHRIST.**

You are a hindrance to me. What a statement! But impartation changed all of that. The man, who at times was a hindrance to Jesus, became the apostle to the Jews after the resurrection. (See Galatians 2:8.)

In fact, on the Day of Pentecost, as thousands of Jews

mocked the believers for being filled with the Holy Spirit, it was Peter who stood to preach the powerful message that resulted in 3,000 salvations that day.

Clearly, impartation doesn't just strengthen and establish you; it makes you useful and productive.

Without a doubt, impartation from one believer to another is clearly demonstrated throughout the New Testament.

As with Timothy, Onesimus, Peter, and many others, impartation empowers you to become what you could not develop into on your own.

It is God's avenue of empowerment for his children, and it's still available today.

THE IMPARTATION OF SOMEONE'S SPIRIT IS AN AVENUE OF PROMOTION IN THE KINGDOM OF GOD. // #FURTHERFASTER

CHAPTER 4

WALKING IN THE POWER OF ANOTHER MAN'S SPIRIT

When the group of prophets from Jericho saw from a distance what happened, they exclaimed, "Elijah's spirit rests upon Elisha!"
– 2 Kings 2:15 NLT

I stood at the altar about to lay hands on people for healing. I was holding one of my first revivals as a young minister.

People had come to the front to receive prayer for sickness, disease, and whatever else was troubling them. Although I had attended many healing services, I'd not conducted many of my own.

Now, standing in front of a partially deaf man, I wondered if I should have conducted any at all.

My flesh was nervous, but I had faith knowing what I had seen God do many times before. The gifts that I had received by impartation would be the key to seeing many more miracles throughout my life.

I grew up traveling on the road with my father and

mother since I was two weeks old. My parents, who are full-time evangelists, held revivals all over America and in other nations. Mighty healing miracles have always marked my father's ministry—and I'd watched them for over twenty years.

Once, when I was a small boy sitting on the front row of one of my dad's miracle services, he prayed for a woman who had a visible tumor.

When it instantly disappeared, I sat forward, pointed my finger, and shouted, "Do it again, Dad!"

> EVEN LEARNING THE METHODS OF MINISTRY IS A FORM OF IMPARTATION YOU CAN RECEIVE.

I'd seen miracle after miracle throughout my lifetime. You couldn't convince me that God doesn't still heal. I'd been watching him do it my entire life.

The question that crept into my mind was whether or not God would use *me* to bring about these miracles.

As I prayed for the people who had come forward during my healing service, I found myself standing in front of a man who was deaf. He had come forward, believing God would open his ears.

I had watched my father minister to the deaf for years. He, in turn, had watched R.W. Schambach, who had watched A.A. Allen. These were all powerful men whose ministries were marked by the miraculous.

I'd seen them all put their fingers in the ears of the deaf and command the spirit that made the person deaf to come out.

This was something they learned from the ministry of Jesus Christ himself:

> *And they brought to him a man who was deaf . . . taking him aside from the crowd privately, he put his fingers into his ears . . . and said to him, "Ephphatha," that is, "Be opened." And his ears were opened . . .*
>
> *Mark 7:32-35 ESV*

As I'll show you later, even learning the *methods of ministry* is a form of impartation. You can learn how to activate the power of God in your own life and ministry by observing those you've served.

I asked the man to remove his hearing aids, reached out, and placed my fingers in his ears. I began to pray and rebuke the deafness and commanded his ears to open.

When I removed my fingers, I knew something had happened. The man's face lit up, and he could hear even a whisper without hearing aids.

I had operated in the same way that I'd seen my father and others operate. Impartation was at work. From that day forward, Carolyn and I have seen many more miracles of healing, deliverance, provision, and protection. The power of God is at work to perform mighty signs and wonders on the earth.

RECEIVING THE POWER OF ANOTHER MAN'S SPIRIT

The concept of walking in someone else's anointing or spirit may seem weird to you or even mystical. I assure you it's not mystical; it's scriptural.

In the Old Testament, two characters stand out to me as an illustration of this fact: Elijah and Elisha. Both men were prophets; however, both weren't on the same level.

Elijah was Elisha's mentor. If you study a bit deeper, you'll find that Elijah wasn't just a prophet, he was a master prophet. Sometimes I refer to him as a *professor* prophet.

This is because Elijah served as a professor for a group known as the Sons of the Prophets. In his notes on 2 Kings 2, Finis J. Dake writes:

> Sons of the prophets were pupils of the prophets, being trained in religious and spiritual matters. They were not a monastic order but a group of

theological students studying the law and the history of God's people, along with sacred poetry and music.

There were several schools of the prophets from the days of Samuel to the New Testament times when Israel was a nation (1 Sam 10:5, 10-12; 19:20, 24).

Elijah was headmaster of several schools — at Gilgal (2 Ki 4:38); at Bethel where Jeroboam had his altar and one of his golden calves (1 Ki 12:29; 13:1-32); at Jericho, and other places (2 Ki 2:3-7,15; 1 Ki 20:35; 21:10).

I inserted that commentary so that you could see that Elijah and Elisha weren't the only prophets on the earth at that time.

Although others received from Elijah, it's fascinating that we only have scriptural evidence of Elisha receiving the power of Elijah's spirit.

As Elijah's ministry was coming to an end, he was taking his final journey and passing through the prophetic campuses one more time.

Each time they encountered the Sons of the Prophets, they came out and spoke condescendingly to Elisha. With what could be viewed as a sarcastic twist, they would question why Elisha could not sense or see that

Elijah was about to be taken away.

Elisha's answer was priceless: "Of course I know, but be quiet about it" (2 Kings 2:3, 5). *Elisha could see what they could see, but he wanted something from Elijah they didn't want.* More on that later.

As Elijah and Elisha came to the Jordan River, Elijah took his mantle and struck the water with it. Immediately, the river parted, and they crossed on dry ground.

When they reached the other side, Elijah asked what final favor he could perform before leaving Elisha.

Elisha's response was supernatural:

> *When they had crossed, Elijah said to Elisha, "Ask what I shall do for you, before I am taken from you." And Elisha said, "Please let there be a double portion of your spirit on me."*
>
> **2 Kings 2:9 ESV**

Did you see that? It seems like an insane thing to ask. Notice that Elisha didn't request a double portion of the Holy Spirit. He asked for a double portion of *Elijah's* spirit — and God wasn't offended.

After Elijah was taken up by a chariot of fire, Elisha picked up his cloak and walked back to the Jordan River. It was the moment of truth.

As he had seen Elijah do moments before, Elisha took the mantle and struck the water, and it parted for him in the same way it parted for Elijah.

As he walked back through the riverbed, the Sons of the Prophets immediately recognized that he was on another level.

> *When the group of prophets from Jericho saw from a distance what happened, they exclaimed, "Elijah's spirit rests upon Elisha!" And they went to meet him and bowed to the ground before him.*
>
> *2 Kings 2:15 NLT*

Something changed so dramatically about Elisha that these men, who mocked him moments before, were now bowing down in front of him.

Not only did they realize the power of the impartation that Elisha had received, but they also recognized him as their new headmaster as Elijah once was.

> *And Elisha came again to Gilgal when there was a famine in the land. And as the sons of the prophets were sitting before him . . .*
>
> *2 Kings 4:38 ESV*

In the same way they had sat and received at the feet of Elijah, they were now receiving at the feet of Elisha. Impartation didn't just give him the ability to operate in the power of his predecessor; it also afforded him supernatural wisdom.

ELIJAH? NEVER MET HIM.

It's interesting to note that Elisha wasn't the only person in the Bible to receive the spirit of Elijah.

John the Baptist, although never having met Elijah (for the apparent reason of being alive hundreds of years later), still received the impartation of his spirit.

> *And [John] will go before [Jesus] in the spirit and power of Elijah, to turn the hearts of the fathers to the children . . .*
> *Luke 1:17 ESV*

This was prophesied by an angel and came to pass in the life of John as he prepared the way for Christ. He never had to meet Elijah to receive an impartation from him. He simply received it by the Word of God.

The same is true for you and me. The things of God are eternal. We don't have to meet certain men and women to receive an impartation from them.

Some of the men I'm receiving from are dead and in Heaven, but their books, audio messages, and videos are still circulating on the earth, and I'm receiving an impartation from them.

Although I'll cover this topic in depth later, always remember that you can receive an impartation directly from the Word of God.

> *And as he spoke to me, the Spirit entered into me and set me on my feet, and I heard him speaking to me.*
> *Ezekiel 2:2 ESV*

Set me on my feet. I love that picture. Just the spoken Word of God can establish you and root you in strength. Ask the Lord to use people that you don't even know to impart spiritual gifts into your life to take you higher.

LEADING BY IMPARTATION

People are very fickle. They can love you one day and hate you the next. Not to mention, they can get very preoccupied with personal cliques and preferences.

If you're a pastor, you'll be able to identify with trying to keep your local body of believers in unity. Because it has been ingrained in humans to be tribe driven for so many centuries, we can quickly identify with a specific group and criticize everyone who isn't a part of it. Yankees or Red Sox? Mac or PC? Coffee or Tea? We can follow the trail down to the smallest things.

This isn't a new concept, either. As the Apostle Paul wrote to the Corinthians, he was quickly tiring of this form of division in the church.

He rebuked them for creating division over whether they followed his ministry or Apollos' ministry.

> *Has Christ been divided into factions?*
> *Was I, Paul, crucified for you? Were any*
> *of you baptized in the name of Paul? Of*
> *course not! I thank God that I did not*
> *baptize any of you . . . for now no one*
> *can say they were baptized in my name.*
> *1 Corinthians 1:13-14 NLT*

It's still common for this to take place in churches. If a congregation gets a new pastor, many times, they will have divided opinions about him.

Inevitably, some will prefer the old pastor who's now gone, and others will be so happy there's a new leader on the scene.

In some cases, I've seen people choose to leave a church they've attended for many years because they simply don't care for the new leadership.

The reason I'm showing you this is so that you will understand how supernatural the transfer between Moses and Joshua was.

Moses had been the leader of Israel for many years. He was the deliverer whom God anointed to bring them out of bondage and toward the Promised Land.

Because of his disobedience, however, he would not be able to complete his journey into Canaan.

God was promoting Joshua to be the new leader of Israel. The only problem was, there were millions of Israelites wandering through the desert, waiting for God's promise.

How would they respond to different leadership? Would this cause a rift among God's people? Would they even make it to the Promised Land under this new regime?

There are churches of two hundred people who can't even agree on which color carpet they should lay in the sanctuary. How did God expect millions of people to fall in line with a new leader *that they didn't even vote on* to lead them into their destiny?

That's where the power of impartation comes in. If Joshua were going to lead Israel into their promise, he would have to have the same spiritual strength that Moses had when he brought them from Egypt.

Moses knew his time was up, and Joshua was God's next man. He took spiritual steps to ensure the transfer of power and wisdom would be complete.

> *Now Joshua son of Nun was full of the spirit of wisdom, for Moses had laid his hands on him. So the people of Israel obeyed him, doing just as the Lord had commanded Moses.*
>
> *Deuteronomy 34:9 NLT*

That is *miraculous! All* of the people (some say as many as 2.5 million) followed Joshua and obeyed his orders.

How was Joshua able to take over right where Moses left off and continue into greater things? It wouldn't have been possible without the power of impartation.

As Elisha leapfrogged past the Sons of the Prophets, Joshua leapfrogged past the other eleven spies that were sent into Canaan to see the land.

I should mention that Joshua wasn't the only spy who had faith. Caleb also returned with a faith-filled report. However, it was the impartation of Moses, coupled with Joshua's faith, that put him in position to be the next leader of Israel.

It's encouraging to know that you don't have to start

from square one. God has given us the ability to walk in the power of another man or woman's spirit.

Seeking impartation seems to be a lost art in our generation, but that's why I'm writing this book. The enemy would love to fill you with pride so that you think you don't need anyone's advice or help, let alone spiritual transfer of power.

We need it. It's God's system of rapid promotion within his Kingdom. God has a plan to promote you beyond what you could accomplish through your own knowledge or strength.

Remember that unless the Lord is building the house, all of our work is worthless (Psalm 127:1). We must recognize that promotion comes from the Lord, and he decided to establish this system of impartation for our benefit. Get ready to be set on another level.

SPIRITUAL MENTORSHIP IS GOD-MADE
NOT MAN-MADE. AVOID IT AT YOUR
OWN RISK. // #FURTHERFASTER

CHAPTER 5

DON'T BE A BASTARD

*For though you have countless guides in Christ, you
do not have many fathers . . .*
– 1 Corinthians 4:15 ESV

Before you get offended by the title of this chapter, let
me explain what it means. The word *bastard* has been
used more recently as a derogatory slang term for a person of whom someone disapproves.

However, I'm using this word in its purest sense to
establish a scriptural truth in this chapter. The dictionary defines *bastard* as "an illegitimate child."

Quite literally, it refers to a child born outside of the
covenant of marriage. In medieval European history,
being a bastard had even more profound consequences.

For example, Henry FitzRoy was the illegitimate son
of King Henry VIII. FitzRoy is an Anglo-Norman surname that means the son of a king.

The surname was attached to children to signify that

they were illegitimate royal offspring (and by others who claimed to be so).[1] One of the downsides to being a bastard is that you were ineligible for succession and, therefore, could not inherit your father's royal office or position.

You were a child who could not take advantage of the family's inheritance because, by legal definition, you weren't a member of that family.

Some monarchs would issue a royal edict legitimizing individual children, but even then, some weren't eligible for succession as was the case for John Beaufort after being legitimized by King Richard II.[2]

KNOWING YOUR IDENTITY AND PURPOSE IS A VITAL PART OF ACHIEVING SUCCESS.

In the Kingdom of God, this principle is true as well. Some are operating as "illegitimate children." That may seem odd as we are all children of God, but as I'm teaching you, God established the system of impartation to empower his people.

You can't be an illegitimate child of God. Either you're born again, or you're not. I'm referring to this principle in the context of having a spiritual father who can impart to you.

One of the many benefits that impartation holds is the revelation of your identity. When I say identity, I'm speaking about your authority and your purpose.

Just as the sons of the prophets immediately recognized Elisha's new identity, we must ask ourselves, "who am I?" Knowing who you are and what you're called to do is a vital part of achieving success in the kingdom of God.

We're not supposed to flounder in a state of confusion; instead, we're called to know God's purpose specifically and pursue it wholeheartedly.

WHO ARE YOU?

After years of serving Evangelist R.W. Schambach, my father has been identified with his ministry more than once. One day, while walking into a grocery store, my father encountered a mother pushing her son out of the store in a wheelchair. He had never met either of them before.

The young man looked to be mentally handicapped and incapacitated. As my father walked by them, the young man sat up—motivated by the demon spirit that oppressed him—and said, "You're Schambach's man!"

His mother became hysterical.

"He spoke!" She shouted. "He's never spoken before." When my father returned home, he called Brother Schambach and told him the story.

"You're not my man," he said. "You're Jesus' man!" Not only can demons sense the anointing on your life, but they can recognize your impartation also.

I want to examine a story found in Acts chapter 19. We see seven men who were sons of a priest named Sceva. They were Jewish exorcists.

One day, these seven men came into contact with a demon-possessed man. Look what they said:

> *Then some of the itinerant Jewish exorcists undertook to invoke the name of the Lord Jesus over those who had evil spirits, saying, "I adjure you by the Jesus whom Paul proclaims."*
>
> *Acts 19:13 ESV*

I want you to notice that they were leaning on a relationship that they didn't have. They had no relationship with Christ, and they had no connection with the Apostle Paul. The demon answered them:

> *But the evil spirit answered them, "Jesus I know, and Paul I recognize, but who are you?"*
>
> *Acts 19:15 ESV*

These men were trying to accomplish supernatural things, but they had no identity in the supernatural realm. The demons did not recognize them.

Please understand that the demon was not just saying he knew who Jesus was; demons truly recognized his identity and position in the spiritual realm.

For example, look at how Legion responds to Jesus' arrival to the region of the Gadarenes:

> *And when [Legion] saw Jesus from afar, he ran and fell down before him. And crying out with a loud voice, he said, "What have you to do with me, Jesus, Son of the Most High God? I adjure you by God, do not torment me."*
>
> *Mark 5:6-7 ESV (Emphasis added)*

Legion, which was a group of many demons, immediately recognized Jesus' identity and power, begging him not to harass them.

The same was true for the Apostle Paul. As he and Silas were in Philippi, they were immediately accosted by a demon-possessed girl who not only recognized their identity but their purpose as well.

By the power of the Holy Spirit, Paul cast the demon out of her, and she was free (Acts 16:16-18).

So, without question, demon spirits can sense your authority and know your identity. When these seven sons of Sceva attempted to take authority over the demon in Acts 19, it didn't recognize them. They were bastards. Look at the sad result:

> *And the man in whom was the evil spirit*
> *leaped on them, mastered all of them and*
> *overpowered them, so that they fled out*
> *of that house naked and wounded.*
>
> *Acts 19:16 ESV*

The demon-possessed man literally beat their clothes off, and they left naked. These men attempted to lean on a relationship that they did not have, *"In the name of Jesus who Paul preaches."*

They weren't personally preaching Christ, nor did they have a relationship with Paul. They merely heard what had been happening through Paul's ministry and attempted to take advantage of it for personal advancement. Personal relationship, however, is crucial.

SENT AS FATHERS

Men of God are sent as fathers to the earth. This was true in the Old and New Testament. We can see the pattern in the Old Testament through the prophets. Even kings of that day referred to prophets as "father."

> *As soon as the king of Israel saw them, he*
> *said to Elisha, "My father, shall I strike*
> *them down? Shall I strike them down?"*
> *2 Kings 6:21 ESV*

Elisha called Elijah his father before he was taken up into Heaven (2 Kings 2:12). It's also interesting to note that the group of prophets in training were called the *sons* of the prophets. (See 2 Kings 2:3.) This is because the prophets took the role as spiritual fathers in their lives.

Elisha, by the power of impartation, naturally replicated the anointing and purpose of his father, Elijah. By God's promotion, he stepped from the role of a son (2 Kings 2:12) into the role of father (2 Kings 6:21). This should be a natural progression in the Body of Christ. Unfortunately, this is not often the case.

As we transition into the New Testament, we can see Jesus modeling the example of sonship with his heavenly Father.

In full submission, he refused to say what his Father did not authorize him to say. (See John 12:49.) Because Jesus never did or said anything his Father didn't permit, he was never illegitimate. As a result, his power flowed freely.

There is a direct connection between the spiritual father and son relationship and the power to accomplish your purpose. The Apostle Paul refers to Timothy as his son multiple times in Scripture.

> *Paul, an apostle of Jesus Christ, by the commandment of God our Savior and the Lord Jesus Christ, our hope, To Timothy, a true son in the faith:*
> *1 Timothy 1:1-2 NKJV*

We know that Paul was not Timothy's natural father because Timothy's father was not Jewish (Acts 16:1), and Paul was a Jew (Acts 21:39).

When Paul refers to Timothy as a son, he uses the Greek word *teknon* rather than *huios,* the more commonly-used term. *Teknon* is used in a metaphorical sense as of a teacher and pupil versus *huios,* which is used for the literal offspring of parents.

In an attempt to discredit the biblical idea of spiritual fathers and sons, some would say that Paul referred to Timothy as his son because he led him to the Lord.

However, Scripture seems to indicate that this is not the case. Acts 16:1-3 tells us that Paul first met Timothy in Lystra. Here, Timothy is already called a disciple (an indication that he was already a Christian).

It's more likely that Timothy was led to the Lord

at a young age by either his grandmother, Lois, or his mother, Eunice, who Paul recognized had already established their faith in Christ (2 Timothy 1:5).

So Paul wasn't Timothy's natural father, nor merely the one who brought about his conversion. He was Timothy's spiritual father and was responsible for his impartation.

Timothy wasn't the only one who could call the Apostle Paul father. As I wrote earlier, Onesimus was one of Paul's spiritual sons as well.

> *I appeal to you for my child, Onesimus, whose father I became in my imprisonment.*
>
> *Philemon 1:10 ESV*

Once again, Paul refers to Onesimus as his *teknon*—figurative or spiritual son. The result of the impartation Paul gave him was evident.

> *Formerly he was useless to you, but now he is indeed useful to you and to me.*
>
> *Philemon 1:11 ESV*

Paul's impartation as a spiritual father changed Onesimus from useless to useful. That's why God ordains fathers in the body of Christ. He wants to establish individuals (and entire congregations as in Romans 1:11) in power and authority.

In an age of spiritual rebellion, when people don't want to receive instruction, many have neglected the impartation that could be obtained if they would connect to those whom God has anointed.

There is a stark contrast between the results of the seven sons of Sceva and the lives of the apostles and their disciples. God doesn't want you to be a spiritual bastard. As Paul wrote to the Corinthians:

> *For though you have countless guides in Christ, you do not have many fathers. For I became your father in Christ Jesus through the gospel. I urge you, then, be imitators of me.*
>
> *1 Corinthians 4:15-16 ESV*

Not only does this passage make it clear that Paul is their spiritual father, it indicates that their relationship is one of training and discipline to make the Corinthians more like Paul and thereby more like Christ.

Impartation is God's system to prepare and equip you for your calling and purpose in his kingdom. As you submit yourself to spiritual authority, you should expect to receive the deposits necessary to quickly and efficiently carry out your calling.

In the following chapters, we're going to examine the methods we must employ to receive the impartation we're seeking.

I pray that through humility and a hunger for the things of God, you will receive a full impartation and accomplish all that God has called you to do with supernatural strength.

PRINCIPLE 1

INTERNAL HONOR

They honor me with their lips,
but their hearts are far from
me. And their worship of me
is nothing . . .

—ISAIAH 29:13 NLT

MANAGE THE CONTENTS OF YOUR HEART.
THEY WILL EVENTUALLY FLOW OUT
OF YOU. // #FURTHERFASTER

CHAPTER 6

As we begin this section on how impartation takes place, we've got to start with the foundational principle of honor. Honor is at the heart of serving. You'll never serve a cause or a person that you dishonor.

But there's a big difference between lip service and what we're calling *internal honor*. By that, I mean honor that begins in your heart.

We mustn't just say the right things publicly. We must truly have an internal sense of honor for the ones from whom we want to receive an impartation.

The Lord spoke through the prophet Isaiah in the Old Testament regarding people who were living like this. He was disappointed with their inward dishonor:

And so the Lord says, "These people say they are mine. They honor me with their lips, but their hearts are far from me. And their worship of me is nothing but man-made rules ...

Isaiah 29:13 NLT

If we want to receive divine impartation from those ahead of us, we must honor them internally. One of the reasons this can be hard is because everyone is human and imperfect. If everyone were perfect, honoring others would never be a struggle.

However, just like living by the fruit of Spirit is a choice that our flesh doesn't want to make, so is honoring others.

HONOR THAT DOESN'T BEGIN IN YOUR HEART IS TEMPORARY AND ULTIMATELY WORTHLESS. IT MUST BE INTERNAL.

The Apostle Paul taught us that we shouldn't evaluate others from a human point of view (2 Corinthians 5:16). The mistake that we may easily make is focusing on someone's imperfect humanity rather than the gift God placed in them.

I'm not encouraging you to ignore sin in someone's life and seek to receive from them anyway. On the contrary, Paul told believers to follow him *as he followed Christ.* (1 Corinthians 11:1) In other words, if I ever stop following Christ, stop following me.

What I mean in this context is that you can't allow your familiarity with a man or woman of God to create dishonor in your heart. You may encounter their humanity and imperfect nature. Continue to honor them when honoring isn't easy.

The reason we must continue with internal honor is that if it is short-circuited, impartation will not take place. This principle was active even in the life of Christ.

> *But Jesus said to them, "A prophet is not without honor except in his own country, among his own relatives, and in his own house." Now He could do no mighty work there, except that He laid His hands on a few sick people and healed them.*
> *Mark 6:4-5 NKJV*

As Jesus went to minister in his hometown, they couldn't get past their familiarity with him, and they dishonored him internally as well as with their words.

What was the result? The Son of God couldn't perform any mighty work there aside from locating the few who did have faith and healing them.

Christ's entire ministry in that region was stifled because of their dishonor. He had miracles to impart to them, but they immediately short-circuited them by their complete lack of honor.

WHY INTERNAL HONOR?

Some of you may be thinking, *why does internal honor matter as long as I take actions of honor and speak honorably?*

The reason honor must originate from your heart is that outward honor—which we'll refer to as *manufactured honor*—can only last so long if it doesn't originate from your heart. Consider this proverb:

> *Above all else, guard your heart, for everything you do flows from it.*
> *Proverbs 4:23 NIV*

You can only fake it for so long before your flesh takes over. Manufactured honor will end, and you will manifest what's really in your heart—dishonor.

> *The good person out of the good treasure of his heart produces good, and the evil person out of his evil treasure produces evil, for out of the abundance of the heart his mouth speaks.*
> *Luke 6:45 ESV*

Here, Jesus is teaching that the thoughts you allow to fill your heart will become the words you speak. Proverbs tells us that we will experience the reality of what we believe in our hearts to be true (Proverbs 23:7).

You can see why honor must begin in your heart and be the foundation for every honorable action that you take.

As Jesus taught, if you don't fill yourself with honor and continue to build that culture in your heart, dishonor will eventually flow out of you.

Manufactured honor is not enough. It's fake and temporary. Furthermore, the passage we read in Isaiah seems to indicate that God is displeased with empty actions of honor that don't originate from your heart.

If the thoughts you have become the words you speak, that will only be the beginning. Eventually, your actions will also be dishonorable, and your connection to the source of impartation will be meaningless.

This is why you must heavily guard impartation relationships and abide by this principle.

THE HONOR KILLERS

When you've found someone who may fill the role of a spiritual father in your life, you must guard that relationship at all costs to continue to receive from them.

Two of the biggest killers of spiritual relationships are gossip and bearing false witness.

The first thing that quickly destroys honor in your heart is listening to gossip. I'm saddened to see how much gossip goes on in the body of Christ today.

When the Apostle Paul is describing wicked people in his letter to the Roman church, he mentions gossips in the same breath as those who hate God and people whose hearts are full of murder (Romans 1:29-30).

As we're learning in this section, gossip is an evil thing that is designed to separate impartation connections. The Word of God assures us that broken relationships will be the result of ongoing gossip:

> *A perverse person stirs up conflict, and a*
> *gossip separates close friends.*
> *Proverbs 16:28 NIV*

The enemy has designed gossip to bring division and disunity into the body of Christ so that he can steal our power and impartation. Because it's a wise thing to seek the power of God by impartation, it is a foolish thing to engage in gossip (Proverbs 10:18).

You have to be proactive in cutting gossip out of your life. More importantly, never entertain gossip from someone else.

That means if someone begins gossiping, you need to shut it down immediately. Just simply tell them that you have no interest in hearing what they have to say about that other person. If they persist, excuse yourself and leave the conversation.

Recently, my pastor, Bishop Rick Thomas, shared a similar story. At one time, he served on a board for the renowned healing evangelist Dr. Oral Roberts.

Because of the dynamic nature of Dr. Roberts' ministry, he had many critics.

Once, while on a flight, a man approached Bishop Thomas out of "concern" for his connection to the supposedly controversial Dr. Oral Roberts. The man wanted to share something he "knew" about Dr. Roberts and warn Bishop Thomas about being connected with him.

> **TWO OF THE BIGGEST KILLERS OF SPIRITUAL RELATIONSHIPS ARE GOSSIP AND BEARING FALSE WITNESS.**

Before the man could get started, Bishop Thomas shut him down, telling him that he didn't care to hear anything the man had to say about his mentor Dr. Roberts. When the man tried to persist, Bishop Thomas assured him that he had two choices: he could return to his seat, or there would be consequences.

Some may think that's a bit harsh. However, now that we understand that God views gossip as wickedness and that it can cancel his plan for your progression in his kingdom, an emphatic response to gossip seems exceedingly appropriate.

Living by principles like these guards us against being disconnected from the power of God. Notice, it doesn't only guard us against losing impartation, but also from losing our very faith.

> *If you claim to be religious but don't control your tongue, you are fooling yourself, and your religion is worthless.*
> *James 1:26 NLT*

King David, who wrote many of the Psalms, knew the importance of pleasing God with his speech. Although he wasn't Spirit-filled as believers are today, he relied on the power of prayer and the assistance of God to make this possible in an Old Testament setting:

> *Set a guard, O Lord, over my mouth; keep watch over the door of my lips!*
> *Psalm 141:3 ESV*

What an eye-opening prayer. David, a man after God's own heart, had a strong desire for God's help to guard his mouth. We can pray that same prayer today and believe for the help of the Spirit in our speech.

The second area that destroys impartation is bearing false witness or lying about others. This is the other area of gossip that poses a dangerous threat to not only our ability to receive impartation but to live holy lives before the Lord. Bearing false witness is a violation of the Ten Commandments.

Although you may think you'd never willingly spread lies about someone else, let me give you an example of how it could easily happen to you by showing you a system I've set up in my own life.

If I hear something about someone that's accompanied by absolutely no evidence, I immediately dismiss it and cut it off.

If I couldn't stand in a courtroom and prove what I'm saying to a judge or jury, I don't say it. (We'll get into whether or not you *should* say it in a moment.)

Receiving second-hand information as truth is one of the most dangerous and harmful things you can do. It's how rumors begin, and gossip is spread.

"Did you hear what she did?" That's how it always begins. When it comes down to the bottom line, it's something someone heard from someone who heard it from someone else.

How do they "know what she did?" Were they there? Did they see it or hear it for themselves? If not, how do we know it happened? *What if it didn't happen?* Now we're participating in lies and false witness.

I want to examine a few biblical rules about what we should do when we have something against someone else in the body of Christ. If Christians lived biblically, it would eliminate so much strife and division in the church. Look what Jesus taught:

> *If your brother sins against you, go and tell him his fault, between you and him alone. If he listens to you, you have gained your brother. But if he does not listen, take one or two others along with you, that every charge may be established by the evidence of two or three witnesses. If he refuses to listen to them, tell it to the church. And if he refuses to listen even to the church, let him be to you as a Gentile and a tax collector.*
>
> *Matthew 18:15-17 ESV*

It always begins with having a personal and private conversation with the one in the wrong. Again, this is someone who has wronged you. That means you know the offense happened, and it's not hearsay or second-hand information.

Furthermore—and this is such a crucial point— charging a brother or sister in Christ is not to be done on a he-said-she-said basis. If they reject your private conversation, bring other Christians along as witnesses that you've done your best to reconcile. Church leaders aren't to be involved until the first two steps have been completed.

Also, other than bringing fellow believers along with you to reconcile with that person, Jesus never taught that other believers should be involved in the knowledge of the offense at all.

Can you see that everything that's being done is in love and with the end goal of reconciliation in mind? It's never to slander or defame a fellow believer.

With the goal of walking in love in mind, ask yourself what result you expect when talking about someone's supposed problem (that you're not even sure happened).

Rather than engaging in gossip and slander, if you somehow hear something negative about a fellow believer, especially a spiritual mentor, don't receive it or repeat it. Pray for those that are over you and ask God to protect and guide them.

God will honor you for honoring them, and you'll never be disconnected from the source of impartation, and your honor will always originate from within—

making it genuine.

As you continue to live an honorable lifestyle, keep in mind that it's a seed you're sowing. You will reap a harvest of honor from others in your life because you live a life of honor. As Paul taught:

> *Repay no one evil for evil, but give thought to do what is honorable in the sight of all. If possible, so far as it depends on you, live peaceably with all.*
> *Romans 12:17-18 ESV*

The writer of Hebrews instructs us to strive for peace and watch out for one another so that we're not corrupted by bitterness (Hebrews 12:14-15).

Begin your journey of impartation by creating a strong foundation of honor in everything you do.

PRINCIPLE 2

BELIEVE IN THE MINISTRY OF THE MAN

Believe in the Lord your God, and you will be established; believe his prophets, and you will succeed.

—2 CHRONICLES 20:20 ESV

YOU WILL NEVER FAITHFULLY SERVE A VISION IN WHICH YOU DO NOT BELIEVE. // #FURTHERFASTER

CHAPTER 7

One day, Elisha, the son of Shaphat (who was a wealthy landowner), was plowing the fields as usual. As he worked, a man was approaching from the direction of Mt. Horeb. It was Elijah the prophet.

During Elijah's time in a cave on top of Mt. Horeb, God instructed him to anoint three people. He was to anoint Hazael to be the King of Syria, Jehu to be the King of Israel, and Elisha to be the prophet *in his place.*

The latter would have to be a miracle. Who would want to leave a wealthy family to become an understudy and live the persecuted life of a prophet?

As Elisha continued to work, Elijah approached him. When he stood next to him, he threw his cloak across Elisha's shoulders. This was an indication that Elisha was to follow Elijah. It was essentially the moment of his calling.

Elisha had a choice at that point. He could have rejected his call and continued working in the field, but he immediately decided to separate from his current lifestyle and pursue his new calling.

Elisha not only pursued his call, but he also took a giant step of faith that would ensure he would continue forward toward his goal.

After Elijah covered him in his cloak, Elisha slaughtered the twenty-four oxen he was using to plow the field, and roasted them on a fire he built with the wood from his plows. Then, Elisha, along with the people of the town, feasted on the meat he cooked.

> "BURNING YOUR PLOWS" MEANS BEING SINGLE-MINDED ABOUT WHAT GOD HAS CALLED YOU TO DO. NO PLAN B.

This action of faith served two important purposes. First, the feast represented a celebration. Elisha wasn't sad to answer his call. It wasn't a time to mourn; it was a time to rejoice. Whenever your call or purpose becomes clear, it's a time to rejoice.

Secondly, this was an action that would force him to move forward in his purpose. Now that his plows were burnt and his oxen all dead, he obviously couldn't go back to farming. There's no need for a backup plan when you follow the plan of God.

How often are we tempted to leave ourselves with a way out just in case what God called us to do doesn't work the way we thought it would?

That's a sign of a lack of faith. It's what the Bible calls being double-minded (James 1:6-8). Those kinds of choices will ensure that the power of God will not operate in your life. As James wrote:

> *For that person must not suppose that he*
> *will receive anything from the Lord;*
> *James 1:7 ESV*

If we want to receive impartation, we must never be confused or doubtful about what we desire to experience in our lives and ministries.

As we'll see shortly, Elisha knew what he wanted to receive from Elijah. That was a factor that turned out to be extremely important in Elisha's life. It set him apart from the rest of the young prophets in training.

Elisha believed in Elijah's ministry enough to forsake everything he'd ever known to follow and serve him. Notice that Elisha's belief in Elijah's ministry took him beyond internal honor to a place of service.

Technically, it's possible to honor someone without believing in their purpose personally. A perfect example of this would be the president of the United States.

Although you may not have voted for him, you still must honor the office of the president. You always treat him with respect and honor because of the position he holds. That doesn't mean you agree with his actions or policies. You may not be a member of his political party, but you can still honor him.

Believing in the purpose is an entirely different matter. Elisha could have honored Elijah on the basis that he was a prophet of God without attaching his own heart to the cause of God.

Others in the Bible honored the prophet Elisha, blessed him, and even received miracles and blessings through him, but never received his impartation.

The wealthy woman from Shunem miraculously had a baby, and then Elisha raised her son from the dead after he died. (See 2 Kings 4.)

However, she didn't become the next prophet after Elisha. She honored him, but she wasn't called to attach her heart to his purpose and receive a full impartation of his ministry.

BELIEF GOES BEYOND

Believing in the ministry of the one from whom you want to receive is the next stop on the road to impartation.

One thing we can see is that Elisha's belief in Elijah's ministry kept him with Elijah. Although other prophets were training in different locations, only Elisha stayed by Elijah's side. Even when Elijah tried to separate Elisha from him, Elisha refused to leave.

On his final journey before being taken up in a chariot of fire, Elijah attempted to separate Elisha from himself. I believe this was a test of Elisha's heart.

> *Elijah said to him, "Elisha, please stay*
> *here, for the Lord has sent me to Jericho."*
> *But he said, "As the Lord lives, and as*
> *you yourself live, I will not leave you."*
> *So they came to Jericho.*
>
> *2 Kings 2:4 ESV*

This test happened three different times before they reached the Jordan River. Elisha successfully passed the test. Notice that none of the other prophets continued with Elijah even though they knew he was about to leave the earth (2 Kings 2:3).

Elisha's belief and the attachment of his heart to the vision and call of Elijah put him in a position to receive the impartation that would be rightfully his.

Don't believe for a moment that following Elijah was always an easy task. I'm sure, like anything else, there were times Elisha felt like quitting.

Elijah, himself, went through seasons in which he battled discouragement because of what was happening all around him.

In fact, during the time Elijah spent in the cave on Mt. Horeb, he was greatly discouraged and crying out to God with the belief that he was the last faithful person that existed.

The worship of Baal had become rampant, and Jezebel was actively murdering the prophets of God. God encouraged Elijah by revealing that he had preserved thousands of people who had never bowed to Baal or kissed him (1 Kings 19:18).

Of course, there was persecution, but that didn't deter Elisha from faithfully following in the footsteps of Elijah until his impartation was complete.

THE BEST DEFENSE IS NO OFFENSE

"The best defense is a good offense" is an adage that's been around for many years. Wrongly attributed to famous Green Bay Packers football coach Vince Lombardi, versions of this mantra have been found as far back as the writings of Sun Tzu

In 1799, George Washington wrote, "make them believe, that offensive operations, often times, is the surest, if not the only (in some cases) means of defence."[1]

The point is that when you're in control and taking action, your enemy has to expend resources dealing with what you're doing rather than launching attacks against you.

In this section, I'm going to slightly modify that mantra to more fully expand your understanding of this chapter's principle.

The best defense is *no* offense. The point I'm making is not about going on the offense, but rather, *taking* offense. Being offended is one of the traps the enemy uses to disconnect your belief from the one with whom God connected you.

> IF THE DEVIL CAN TRICK YOU INTO BEING OFFENDED, HE CAN KEEP YOU FROM THE IMPARTATION THAT GOD HAS PLANNED FOR YOUR LIFE.

The best defense against losing the impartation that God planned for your life is by taking no offense.

A perfect example of this principle is found in the Old Testament. Before taking the Promised Land for themselves, Israel had to send spies into Canaan to get a full report of what to expect.

Moses chose a man from each of the twelve tribes and appointed them as the spies for this mission. I want to highlight two of the twelve men — Caleb, who represented the tribe of Judah, and Joshua, who represented the tribe of Ephraim.

The reason I'm emphasizing these two men is that they were the only ones who returned from the Promised Land with a report of faith. The rest of the men returned in fear.

When they arrived home ready to give their description of the land to Moses and the rest of Israel, the ten men who had an evil report talked about the giants and how powerful they were. They assured Moses that Israel was too insignificant to take the land.

Joshua and Caleb were different. They had a confession of faith, which they conveyed clearly.

> *Do not rebel against the Lord, and don't*
> *be afraid of the people of the land. They*
> *are only helpless prey to us! They have*
> *no protection, but the Lord is with us!*
> *Don't be afraid of them!*
> *Numbers 14:9 NLT*

Although Joshua and Caleb had faith, the people of Israel believed the report of fear instead. This brought about the judgment of the Lord, and they wandered outside of their promise for forty-five more years. Caleb grew tired of waiting around.

> *I am still as strong today as I was in*
> *the day that Moses sent me; my strength*
> *now is as my strength was then, for war*
> *and for going and coming.*
>
> *Joshua 14:11 ESV*

Joshua was still around as well. He never lost his faith, either. God was about to promote him to be the leader of Israel. He would take over where Moses finished. Joshua ended up receiving a full impartation from Moses so that all the people of Israel followed him as they did Moses.

Here's a powerful lesson from this story. When Joshua returned from Canaan with a report of faith, he knew that immediately taking the Promised Land was God's desire for Israel.

He and Caleb were so distraught when the people of Israel decided to rebel that they tore their clothes to show their grief and rebuked the congregation.

However, when Israel didn't go the way Joshua knew they should, he didn't get offended and leave. He believed in the ministry of Moses. He stayed and was faithful to God.

If Joshua had become offended that no one believed his report and left, it would have disqualified him from receiving the impartation from Moses.

How interesting that Caleb was still among the tribes following the commands of Moses forty-five years later.

How many people do you think would stay faithful for four decades in the same conditions?

Joshua refused to be offended because of what happened. He stayed faithful until he received a full impartation from Moses. In fact, it was Joshua, not Moses, who was blessed with the right to lead Israel into their Promised Land. His inability to be offended brought him into great promotion through impartation.

THE FOUNDATION OF THE CHURCH

Interestingly, this powerful principle was the foundation of the New Testament church.

In a time when everyone had different opinions about who Jesus was (though he had plainly explained his identity), Peter recognized him perfectly.

Some were saying that Jesus was John the Baptist or Elijah, and others said Jeremiah or one of the prophets. Jesus asked his disciples who they thought he was.

> *Simon Peter replied, "You are the Christ,*
> *the Son of the living God."*
> *Matthew 16:16 ESV*

Jesus blessed Peter for his response and told him that human wisdom couldn't have taught him this truth. God is the one who revealed it to Peter.

Then, after blessing Peter, Jesus described the power of Peter's divine revelation from Heaven. What Peter knew became the foundation of the church.

> *And I tell you, you are Peter, and on this*
> *rock I will build my church, and the gates*
> *of hell shall not prevail against it.*
> *Matthew 16:18 ESV*

This verse has been improperly used by the Roman Catholic Church to establish the fact that Peter was the first pope. That isn't what Jesus was saying.

It's helpful to look at the Greek words used in the verse to fully understand what Jesus meant. Jesus began by saying, "you are Peter." The Greek word translated Peter is the word *petros,* which means a *piece* of rock.

Then, Jesus said, "and upon this rock I will build my church . . ." The Greek word translated rock is *petra,* which means a *mass* of rock.

Jesus wasn't saying that he would build the church upon Peter; it would be built upon the revelation of who Christ was! Consider this verse:

This Jesus is the stone that was rejected by you, the builders, which has become the cornerstone.

Acts 4:11 ESV

Peter's revelation of Christ—his belief in the ministry of the man—was what enabled him to receive impartation from Jesus. Furthermore, this impartation isn't limited to Peter. Anyone who receives the revelation Peter had will also receive the impartation of Christ.

But to all who did receive him, who believed in his name, he gave the right to become children of God,

John 1:12 ESV

Why would Peter continue to serve Christ and his ministry long after Jesus' death and eventually die for it if he didn't believe in the ministry of the man?

Even Paul, who was not one of Jesus' original twelve apostles, gained the revelation that Christ was the cornerstone of the church (Ephesians 2:20).

If we are going to receive impartation, it's not enough to just honor the one who carries it. We must fully believe in the ministry of that man or woman.

FULL IMPARTATION

As I showed you in this chapter, our belief in the ministry of another will take us beyond honor and into service. Serving another is truly the catalyst for receiving a *full* impartation.

Have you noticed that at different points throughout the book, I've intentionally used the term *full impartation?* There's a crucial reason for that.

As I defined in the first chapter, impartation simply means to bestow a quality or attribute that was not previously there.

Anything you receive supernaturally as a gift is imparted to you. However, just because you received a spiritual endowment from someone doesn't mean you received their full impartation. Let me explain.

When Elijah visited the widow of Zarephath during the terrible drought that he prophesied, he was there to bless her supernaturally.

If you know the story, she was about to cook her last meal and then die. After Elijah finished ministering to her, she had a miraculous, never-ending supply of flour and oil until the drought ended.

Elijah imparted that gift to her by the anointing. However, that woman didn't receive a full impartation from Elijah and become the prophet after him.

Just like the woman from Shunem didn't become Elisha's successor. So there is impartation, and then there is *full* impartation.

In Scripture, impartation seems to encompass miracles of healing, provision, strength, revelation knowledge, etc., whereas full impartation appears to be linked to someone's calling or purpose.

For example, I have received many wonderful impartations from different men of God around the world. However, that doesn't mean that I've become their spiritual son and will assume their role in ministry when they leave the earth.

After careful Bible study, it would seem we'd be foolish to assume we could receive a full impartation from someone without first serving them.

Though many supernatural benefits can be imparted to members of the body of Christ (as Paul seems to indicate in Romans 1:11), full impartation comes through faithful service over a period of time as in the cases of Elisha, Joshua, Peter, Timothy, Titus, Onesimus, and many others.

We will never seek to serve if we don't believe in the ministry we're serving. Let the heart of a servant become your defining characteristic. (See Matthew 20:26.)

PRINCIPLE 3

CRAVE WHAT HE CARRIES

*But earnestly desire the
higher gifts. And I will show
you a still more excellent way.*

—1 CORINTHIANS 12:31 ESV

SPIRITUAL HUNGER DRIVES SPIRITUAL ACTIONS. THAT'S WHY THE DEVIL IS INTO STARVATION. // #FURTHERFASTER

CHAPTER 8

Alfred Howard Carter, better known as Howard Carter, was indeed a pioneer of the Pentecostal movement in Great Britain and around the world.[1]

Carter was born in Birmingham, England, in 1891 and was born again in 1909 at the age of eighteen.

At twenty-four years old, he was filled with the Spirit and began his ministry. By then, World War I had broken out against England, but Howard Carter didn't feel that he should take up arms against others as he was a minister.

England didn't allow conscientious objectors, and so he was thrown into Wormwood Scrubs prison in west London. Later, Carter spent time in Princetown Work Centre, which was formerly Dartmoor Prison.[2]

It was during this time in prison that God met with Carter and gave him a divine revelation on the gifts of the Holy Spirit. God showed him that the gifts were supernatural and not natural.

Until that time, many believed that the word of knowledge was natural knowledge as a college professor would have. Many also thought that the gift of healing was facilitated by medical doctors.[3]

When he was released from prison, he began teaching these truths about the gifts of the Spirit everywhere. In 1921, he became the headmaster of Hampstead Bible School—a position that he held for twenty-seven years.[4]

He also became a founding member and chairman of the Assemblies of God in Great Britain and Ireland.[5]

One day, Howard was praying in one of London's grey, stone churches. After spending a few hours in meditation, he heard the voice of the Lord speak:

"Arise, thou my servant, and prepare for the journey; let not another send thee, for I shall send thee and supply all thy needs. Arise, and go, be a blessing to my people in the uttermost parts of the earth."

So, in 1948, he left Hampstead Bible School and England behind and moved to the United States.[6]

For the final twenty-seven years of his life, he traveled the world and preached the gospel. This is where the story gets fascinating.

A JOURNEY ON BLIND FAITH

God didn't send Howard Carter around the world by himself. He appointed a young man to help and serve him — Lester Sumrall.

As they traveled the world together, Howard Carter (who was a strict statistician) estimated that they traveled one thousand miles per week.

They traveled on every type of transportation you can imagine, from airplanes to chairs carried by natives at three miles per hour.

They preached the gospel in eighteen languages with the assistance of sixty-five different interpreters seeing miracles and conversions in many nations of the world.

This kind of impact through apostolic power was Sumrall's heart's cry. His greatest desire, like Carter, was to be a blessing to his generation.

Dr. Sumrall (as he was later referred to) wrote in his captivating book *Adventuring with Christ*:

> If only [I] could live as long as Methuselah, with the patience of Job, the faith of Abraham, the bravery of David, and with the purity of Christ, he might come to understand the mystery of it all-then die content, having been a blessing to mankind.[7]

When Howard Carter first met Lester Sumrall in Eureka Springs, Arkansas, brother Carter had a prophetic word that he and Lester Sumrall were to travel the world together.

Shortly afterward, as Sumrall was acquiring his passport, Howard Carter was finishing speaking engagements in Australia. They planned to meet one another in Hong Kong.

Dr. Sumrall had purchased his ticket and had his baggage placed on board the ship for China when a special letter arrived from Carter.

"Don't sail for China," it read. "Come to Australia. New developments have changed our itinerary. An invitation to Java for two months also open doors in New Zealand."

Dr. Sumrall didn't know what to do. It was only two days before his voyage to China, and steamship companies weren't in the habit of refunding money that close to departure. Furthermore, he had no money for an additional ticket.

Dr. Sumrall prayed, his money was miraculously refunded, and two days later, he was boarding a steamship bound for Australia.

No one was sponsoring his trip or providing his finances. He left the dock with $12 in his pocket and spiritual hunger filling his soul.

When he arrived at the harbor in Australia, all passengers received declaration forms that they had to fill out and submit to immigration.

The form requested that you specify how much money you were traveling with and gave a warning. "If you are a foreigner staying in Australia for three months, you must have £200."

Dr. Sumrall left the space blank and went to see the immigration officer. There was an American passenger ahead of him who was only traveling with $75.

"We don't want beggars in Australia," said the officer. "Give me your passport and ticket; we are going to send you back to America on the next boat!"

When Dr. Sumrall stood before the officer, the form identified him as a minister. The officer asked him the same question. When he replied that he only had $12, the officer asked where he was going to minister next.

"I am going around the world to preach the gospel to those that have never accepted Christ as their Savior. I am going to Java, Singapore, China, Manchuria, Korea, Japan, and the Lord will provide," he replied.

After studying him for a moment in silence, the Chief Inspector said, "We're going to let you land."

A few days later, on January 1st, Dr. Sumrall arrived in Sydney, where he embraced Carter in the customs shed of the pier.

It had now been five months since the night Dr. Sumrall had received that prophetic word from Howard Carter. What would cause a man to travel thousands of miles to unfamiliar lands, spend all of his money (with no natural guarantee of more), and still be excited at the end of it all?

Spiritual hunger.

Dr. Sumrall very clearly craved the anointing Howard Carter carried as a man of God. Not only did he honor him, he believed in his ministry.

However, he could have stopped there. He could have believed in Carter from afar. There was another step in the process that allowed Dr. Sumrall to receive a full impartation from Carter—hunger.

HUNGER = DESIRE

Honor and belief both acknowledge the anointing of a man's ministry. This third step of hunger craves what that man has.

This is a scriptural principle. The Apostle Paul instructed the church to *covet* the gifts of the Spirit. (See 1 Corinthians 12:31.) The Greek word translated covet means to be envious or jealous over.

Simply stated, it's not wrong to want impartation or spiritual gifts—it's right!

Why would Joshua overrule his flesh's tendency to be angry or offended and leave when Moses and the people didn't believe his report of faith? Hunger for what Moses had.

Why would Elisha be willing to kill his oxen and burn his plows while giving up the inheritance of his wealthy family? Hunger for what Elijah had.

Why would the disciples be willing to endure persecution and hardship when they could have easily abandoned Christ's ministry? Hunger for what Jesus had.

Why did Timothy patiently submit to Paul's instruction and guidance even when he probably felt unqualified to lead those in his church? He had an intense hunger for what Paul had.

I could continue to make examples of men in Scripture who received impartation because they had a strong desire to receive what someone carried, but before I go further, I want to warn you of a dangerous mistake.

THE GUILLOTINE OF GREED

As we're discussing a rarely-taught topic, it's essential to realize that it's also an improperly-taught topic. It's a subject that has been heavily abused throughout the years. Because there are very few books written about impartation (I had a hard time finding any), I want to ensure that I cover the abuses as well as the blessings so that no one is deceived.

One of the first attempted abuses we see in Scripture takes place in the Old Testament. In Numbers chapter 22, Balak, King of Moab, was disturbed by the Israelites because they had already defeated two kings near his region. Fearing that he would be next, he contacted a prophet named Balaam.

Balak tried to pay Balaam to curse God's people. The money tempted Balaam, and although he knew he could only say what God told him to say, he attempted to persuade the Lord to allow him to curse the Israelites by offering multiple sacrifices.

Balaam even participated in divination and witchcraft in an attempt to receive Balak's reward. God not only rebuked him, but ultimately, the Spirit of the Lord left him, and he continued as a soothsayer operating in witchcraft (Joshua 13:22).

The Apostle Peter describes false teachers who pervert the anointing in the same way:

> *They are well trained in greed. They live under God's curse . . . They have followed the footsteps of Balaam son of Beor, who loved to earn money by doing wrong.*
> *2 Peter 2:14-15 NLT*

We are never to desire impartation of spiritual gifts so that we can use them for monetary gain. As Peter said, using spiritual gifts for profit is a sure way to attract the curse of God upon your life.

Although God will financially bless you for your obedience to his call upon your life, you should never use God's holy anointing to manipulate financial gain.

Sadly, one of the things that is still seen in today's culture is the pay-for-prophecy hucksters. These false prophets and teachers would have you believe that if you'll contact them and give a certain amount of money, it will unlock a personal prophecy for your life. You might as well call a psychic hotline.

These are servants of the devil, and if they don't repent, they will be harshly judged one day.

You never have to pay money to receive a word from the Lord. The Holy Spirit, who guides you into all truth, lives in you. You have communion with him and can hear from him at any time.

THE POWER CAN'T BE PURCHASED

On the other side of this error is the thought that you can pay to operate in the power of God. If you have kids, you know that many of the games that are available for our phones and tablets have what's known as "in-app purchases." Though the game may be free to download, the developers have weaseled $50 out of you for gems, blind boxes, points, outfits for your avatars, etc.

Many times, these same things can be unlocked simply by playing the game more often. However, as you know, our kids don't want to wait to unlock the next thing. They want you to approve a $1.99 purchase for a box of gems or whatever intangible benefit the game offers.

I think some Christians believe they can upgrade the power of the Spirit in their lives by "purchasing an upgrade."

I want to be clear that I'm not speaking against sowing financial seed and believing for increase. The system of seedtime and harvest is biblical and will always be in operation. However, one thing that's important to remember about the system is this:

> *Do not be deceived: God is not mocked, for whatever one sows, THAT will he also reap.*
> *Galatians 6:7 ESV (Emphasis added)*

Notice that the type of seed you sow always determines the kind of harvest you'll reap. When I was a young boy, I heard the phrase, "If you want to have friends, show yourself friendly." That's an example of this principle in operation. Apple seeds produce apple trees. Friendliness provokes friendship. Financial seeds reap a financial harvest. We should never believe that we can buy the power of God—our impartation—with money.

In Acts chapter 8, Philip had left Jerusalem and arrived in Samaria. After preaching the gospel and performing miracles, many were saved, healed, and delivered from demons.

> THE POWER OF GOD CANNOT BE PURCHASED AND IT CAN NEVER BE SOLD. WE RECEIVE IT BY FAITH.

There was a sorcerer named Simon who lived there. He practiced magic, amazed the people of Samaria, and claimed to be great.

When Philip preached the gospel, Simon believed it, was baptized, and began to follow Philip. Simon was utterly amazed by the miracles which Philip performed.

After so many people had been converted, Peter and John were sent to Samaria from Jerusalem so that the new believers would be filled with the Holy Spirit.

They began laying hands on the believers, and they were baptized in the Holy Spirit. When Simon saw this, he offered the apostles money to have the same kind of power.

What we can see about Simon from Scripture is that he had a severe problem with pride. He loved to amaze the people of Samaria with magic, and if that wasn't enough, he constantly claimed to be a great man. He hadn't dealt with the sin of pride during his short time as a believer.

The sad truth is that if he had humbly followed the apostles' teaching, he would have learned that every Spirit-filled believer can lay their hands on others and impart the gift of the Holy Spirit. Instead, he tried to buy it. Peter rebuked him:

> *"May your money be destroyed with you for thinking God's gift can be bought! You can have no part in this, for your heart is not right with God. Repent of your wickedness and pray to the Lord. Perhaps he will forgive your evil thoughts, for I can see that you are full of bitter jealousy and are held captive by sin."*
>
> *Acts 8:20-23 NLT*

It's a harsh correction that Simon received from Peter. Notice that Peter tells Simon that his heart is wicked. It's a very evil thing to think we can purchase the anointing of God with money.

There is a price to be paid. Just like our children want to unlock new treasures by purchasing upgrades rather than faithfully playing their games, many aren't willing to pay the price of faithfulness to the anointing of God. Those who want the quick way are usually those who don't have the character to endure in the long run.

Never allow the desire for riches or the pride of being used by God's power to guide your decisions in your journey to receiving impartation.

FAITH HAS A VISION

As you hunger for the things of the Spirit, you must know what you desire. Faith has to have a target. We can't flounder in uncertainty. Paul writes:

> *Do not be anxious about anything, but in everything by prayer and supplication with thanksgiving let your requests be made known to God.*
>
> *Philippians 4:6 ESV*

Make your requests known. To voice them, you must know them. When Jesus was leaving Jericho in Mark chapter 10, he heard the cry for mercy from Bartimaeus.

When Jesus called for Bartimaeus, he asked him a very simple question. The important thing was that Bartimaeus had an answer.

> *"What do you want me to do for you?"*
> *And the blind man said to him, "Rabbi,*
> *let me recover my sight."*
>
> *Mark 10:51 ESV*

Bartimaeus called to Jesus as he was leaving Jericho because he *believed* Jesus could heal him, and he *desired* that impartation enough to cry out for Christ.

As he revealed his faith, Jesus answered with an impartation of the miraculous. Instantly, Bartimaeus' eyes opened, and he could see.

Similarly, when it came time for Elisha to voice his desire to Elijah, he was ready with spiritual hunger.

> *When they had crossed, Elijah said to El-*
> *isha, "Ask what I shall do for you, before*
> *I am taken from you." And Elisha said,*
> *"Please let there be a double portion of*
> *your spirit on me."*
>
> *2 Kings 2:9 ESV*

Elisha wasn't bashful or uncertain. He knew exactly what he wanted from Elijah. Even though by Elijah's admission, it was a hard thing, they both knew they served the God of the impossible.

It may be possible that God viewed Elisha as Elijah's

"firstborn spiritual son," and that was why he had access to a double portion inheritance of Elijah's spirit.

This law is documented for natural-born sons in the book of Deuteronomy:

> *But he shall acknowledge the firstborn,*
> *the son of the unloved, by giving him a*
> *double portion of all that he has, for he*
> *is the firstfruits of his strength. The right*
> *of the firstborn is his.*
>
> *Deuteronomy 21:17 ESV*

Whatever the case may be, we know that Elisha's honor, belief, and hunger brought him into a double portion of Elijah's spirit, and he finished his ministry performing twice as many miracles as Elijah.

The same must be true for you. Don't be too timid to declare what you're believing. This doesn't mean continually claiming that you're in line to receive someone's anointing or mantle.

Know it internally and press forward in humility, serving and receiving from those who are over you. God will reward you for your hunger.

One of the verses that I love to quote is found in Jesus' Sermon on the Mount. Every time I meditate on it, I feel the inherent power that's found in spiritual hunger.

*Blessed are those who hunger and thirst
for righteousness, For they shall be filled.*
Matthew 5:6 NKJV

Notice the prerequisite for being filled. It's always hunger. In his book, *Spiritual Hunger*, missionary Apostle John G. Lake wrote:

> [Hunger] is the greatest persuader I know of. It is a marvelous power. Nations have learned that you can do almost anything with a populace until they get hungry. But when they get hungry, watch out. There is a certain spirit of desperation that accompanies hunger. I wish we all had it spiritually. I wish we were desperately hungry for God. Wouldn't it be glorious?[8]

If you study the lives and ministries of men who changed the world, you'll find that they all had one thing in common — they were all very hungry for the power of God.

PRINCIPLE 4

TAKE ADVANTAGE OF PHYSICAL CONTACT

And Joshua the son of Nun was full of the spirit of wisdom, for Moses had laid his hands on him.

—DEUTERONOMY 34:9 ESV

YOU CAN RECEIVE IN ONE TOUCH WHAT'S NOT AVAILABLE IN AN ENTIRE LIBRARY OF BOOKS. // #FURTHERFASTER

CHAPTER 9

I grew up in the Pentecostal movement. As a young boy, I was in revival services almost every night while my father and mother ministered across the country and around the world.

I loved hearing the gospel music that was a staple of these Holy Ghost meetings. Even as we traveled from state to state, dad would play cassette tapes of the classic gospel greats.

We listened to Andrae Crouch, Walter Hawkins, Gene Martin, Mahalia Jackson, and many others. Early on, I was drawn to the drums (as most young boys in church are). When services would end, I'd hop on and beat them the first chance I got.

When I got a bit older, my father began to help Evangelist R.W. Schambach as he ministered under the tent in the inner cities of America. It was then that I truly fell in love with the instrument that defines gospel music — the B3 Hammond organ.

Anointed praise and worship punctuated the beginning of the service every night. They always kept the volume at a level that would escape the tent and fill the city neighborhoods. People would wander in just to investigate the music.

I'd take a position on the front row (getting as close to the music as I could), and dance until the music ended. I wanted to get closer.

When I finally built up the courage, I'd start standing to the side of the platform near the Leslie speaker. For the uninitiated, a Leslie is a big speaker encased in a wooden cabinet that's connected to a Hammond organ.

After a few nights of that, I snuck up the stairs and stood behind Willie Isaac, R.W. Schambach's organist, while he played.

Finally, I was sitting on the organ bench right next to him, watching his hands and feet as the organ screamed. I can remember Brother Schambach would come onto the platform, look over, and just shake his head and laugh — but he never made me leave.

Brother Schambach would always finish those ten-day tent crusades with a Sunday afternoon children's blessing service in which he'd pray a nine-part blessing on every child who came through the prayer line.

It was in one of those services that I received a supernatural impartation that changed me forever.

As I came through the prayer line with all the other kids, Brother Schambach stopped me when I got in front of him. He laid hands on me and asked the Lord to give me the desire of my heart to play gospel music on the keyboard and organ.

From that day forward, the Lord anointed my mind, and I began to play. Shortly after that, I formed a praise and worship team in my youth group and began to lead worship every week.

At the time of this writing, I've been leading praise and worship for twenty-one years. That gift has taken me around the world and has been instrumental in seeing signs and wonders take place.

To this day, I've never had one piano lesson. I've studied to increase my gift, as the Bible teaches, but I have no formal training. Impartation took me further faster than I could have gotten on my own.

TRANSFORMATION THROUGH TOUCH

If you're reading this and you're relatively new to Pentecostal Christianity, the basis of this chapter may seem odd to you. I assure you, however, that this is not some new doctrine or fad that has recently appeared. On the contrary, the transfer of power through physical contact is something that is seen in Scripture as early as the book of Genesis.

We could argue that the very first time we see the laying on of hands in the Bible was when Jacob wrestled with God in Genesis chapter 32.

From that day forward, God blessed Jacob and changed his name to Israel. He was no longer Jacob the deceiver; he was Israel — a man who had wrestled with God and prevailed.

Years later, when it was time to bless his grandsons, Jacob stretched out his hands and touched their heads to transfer the blessing onto their lives.

Joseph brought Manasseh (the firstborn) and Ephraim (his younger child) to Jacob. Typically, the greater blessing would go to the firstborn. However, when Jacob began to prophesy over them, he crossed his hands and laid his right hand on the younger boy and his left hand on the firstborn.

This shows us that birthright alone did not determine the covenant blessing of increase. It was impartation that was the catalyst for the blessing.

It was extremely unorthodox to bless the younger boy with the blessing of the firstborn. It irritated Joseph, and he tried to reposition his father's hands, but his father refused.

> *"I know, my son; I know," he replied. "Manasseh will also become a great people, but his younger brother will become even greater . . .*
>
> *Genesis 48:19 NLT*

The impartation of the blessing ensured that the younger son would become even greater than his older brother.

The transfer of power and blessing through physical touch is well documented throughout Scripture. In the previous two examples, We see life-altering blessing imparted through touch. Jesus also used this method to transfer spiritual blessing in the New Testament.

Once, parents brought their children to Jesus so that he would lay hands on them, but the disciples scolded the parents for bothering Jesus. Jesus rebuked them for trying to keep the children away from him.

> *But Jesus said, "Let the children come to me . . . And he placed his hands on their heads and blessed them before he left.*
>
> *Matthew 19:14-15 NLT*

We can see that spiritual blessing can be transferred through the avenue of physical contact. God is so interested in his children partaking in the plan of redemption that he made this method of impartation a mandatory system for us.

HEALING IN YOUR HANDS

When Jesus gave us the Great Commission, he didn't only tell us to preach the gospel; he described the signs and wonders that would follow his witnesses.

> *And these signs will accompany those who believe: in my name they will cast out demons; they will speak in new tongues . . . they will lay their hands on the sick, and they will recover.*
> *Mark 16:17-18 ESV*

Jesus commanded us to lay our hands on the sick and impart healing and divine life into their bodies.

Many people wonder how this is possible. Why should we expect someone to be healed when we touch them and pray?

First, because Jesus commanded us to do it. Anything God commands, he empowers. God does what he said he would do. Balaam, the prophet, said it in such a powerful way when he addressed King Balak:

> *God is not a man, so he does not lie. He is not human, so he does not change his mind. Has he ever spoken and failed to act? Has he ever promised and not carried it through?*
>
> *Numbers 23:19 NLT*

God's Word is so powerful that it can never be rendered void or null. It always performs what he sends it to do. (See Isaiah 55:11.)

So if Christ promised us healing would take place when we lay hands on the sick, it will happen.

The second reason we can expect this to happen is that Christ promised us that we would carry on his ministry and purpose because we represent his body.

Part of becoming a son of God is gaining the ability to do the works that Christ did.

> *I tell you the truth, anyone who believes in me will do the same works I have done, and even greater works, because I am going to be with the Father.*
>
> *John 14:21 NLT*

When Jesus said, "because I am going to be with the Father," he was referring to the fact that he was going to send us the Holy Spirit.

Just a few verses later, Jesus says that he will then ask the Father, and he will send us a Comforter (the Holy Spirit) who will lead and guide us into all truth (John 14:16-17).

Jesus wanted us to understand that once the Holy Spirit dwells within us, we will be empowered to do exactly what he did.

Peter and John had spent enough time with Jesus to understand that the power of divine healing could be transferred to others by laying hands on them.

They knew that they were carriers of the Holy Spirit's power. Furthermore, they knew they could transfer this power to others.

This is seen in Acts chapter 3 when they encounter a lame man begging near the temple. When the beggar asked them for money, Peter's answer reveals his understanding of the power they carried:

> *But Peter said, "I have no silver and gold, but WHAT I DO HAVE I give to you. In the name of Jesus Christ of Nazareth, rise up and walk!"*
>
> *Acts 3:6 ESV (Emphasis added)*

Peter and John didn't wonder if they had the Holy Spirit's power within them. They *knew* it. That knowledge led them to take immediate action in obedience to Christ's commands.

As they obeyed the Great Commission, the power of God immediately began to work.

> *And he took him by the right hand and*
> *raised him up, and immediately his feet*
> *and ankles were made strong.*
> *Acts 3:7 ESV*

Notice that at the very moment they took him by the hand, his feet and ankles received strength. That strength was imparted to him by those believers.

It's also valuable to point out that they didn't lay their hands on the man's head. Sometimes we get so caught up in religious traditions that we think God can only manifest his power in one way.

Let's not forget that Elisha laid his entire body on a dead boy, eye to eye, mouth to mouth, hand to hand to raise him from the dead (2 Kings 4:34).

Jesus simply touched a casket that held a dead boy (not his body), spoke, and the boy came back to life.

When I was a student at Rhema Bible Training Center in Tulsa, Oklahoma, I was heavily involved in the

Prayer and Healing Center. These services were conducted daily throughout the week. Many sick people would attend these services, and some were brought from the hospital seeking healing.

As we relied on the Word of God and the anointing of his Spirit, many miracles took place with reported testimonies.

We were taught the principle that I'm teaching you now. You don't have to formally lay your hands on someone's forehead to impart healing.

> **HEALING IS TRANSFERRED THROUGH YOUR HANDS BECAUSE YOUR HANDS ARE CHRIST'S HANDS.**

Even the ushers and greeters were encouraged to believe God that when they shook hands with or hugged those attending the services, that healing virtue would be transferred into their bodies.

One example sticks out in my mind twenty years later. One of the ushers shook hands with a man who came to receive prayer for stage four cancer.

No one else laid hands on the man that day. The handshake was the only contact he received. I remember when he returned with his testimony. He was free from cancer. We praised God like it was our own personal miracle.

God ordained physical touch as a method to expedite

impartation, and in this case, the impartation of divine healing. Never doubt what's possible when you simply obey God's Word.

GIFTS, CALLING, & PURPOSE

We see that spiritual blessings and divine healing can be imparted through physical touch, but what about spiritual gifts?

We've already established that spiritual gifts can and should be imparted, but let's take a look at *how* they are imparted.

As I've written, the leadership transition between Moses and Joshua wasn't just amazing; it was miraculous. To see millions of people immediately shift their allegiance to a new leader is unheard of.

The Word of God tells us why this miracle was possible and how it took place:

> *Now Joshua son of Nun was full of the spirit of wisdom, for Moses had laid his hands on him. So the people of Israel obeyed him, doing just as the Lord had commanded Moses.*
>
> *Deuteronomy 34:9 NLT*

It was impartation through physical touch that brought the spirit of wisdom to Joshua. This imparted spiritual gift allowed Joshua to fulfill his calling and purpose successfully.

When Saul (who was later Paul) and Barnabas were commissioned for the work of the ministry, this was the method that marked their calling and purpose, as well.

> *The Holy Spirit said, "Now separate to Me Barnabas and Saul for the work to which I have called them." Then, having fasted and prayed, and laid hands on them, they sent them away.*
> *Acts 13:2-3 NKJV*

Here, the Greek word translated "separate" actually means to appoint for a purpose or to mark off from others by boundaries.

As hands were laid on Paul and Barnabas, the power of God appointed them to their purpose and calling, and they began their ministries.

Later, we see that Paul continues in God's method of impartation for believers and men of God. Notice what he writes to the church in Rome. He has a plan to bring strength to the entire body of believers:

> *For I long to see you, that I may impart*
> *to you some spiritual gift to strengthen*
> *you.*
> > *Romans 1:11 ESV*

Without question, Paul continued using the power of impartation to transfer spiritual gifts to the church to strengthen them. The question is, how did he do it? We see the answer in his interactions with his son in the faith—Timothy.

> *For this reason I remind you to fan into*
> *flame the gift of God, which is in you*
> *through the laying on of my hands,*
> > *2 Timothy 1:6 ESV*

Timothy is an interesting example because he came from a household of faith. Paul references this fact as he encourages Timothy.

> *I am reminded of your sincere faith, a*
> *faith that dwelt first in your grandmoth-*
> *er Lois and your mother Eunice and now,*
> *I am sure, dwells in you as well.*
> > *2 Timothy 1:5 ESV*

Paul is making a clear distinction between the generational faith imparted to Timothy through his mother and grandmother, and the spiritual gifts that now resided in Timothy through the laying on of his hands. Paul was able to transfer gifts to Timothy that would strengthen and establish him in the ministry.

The laying on of hands isn't limited to spiritual blessing, divine healing, or the baptism of the Holy Spirit. It functions to appoint believers to their purpose and equip them with spiritual gifts that empower them to fulfill that purpose with accuracy.

IMPARTATION FLOWS DOWN

Taking advantage of opportunities to access impartation through the laying on of hands is a wise thing to do. Since it is an avenue established by God, we should actively pursue it.

Some may find this odd, but it's important to remember the principle that God spoke through Isaiah:

> *For as the heavens are higher than the earth, so are my ways higher than your ways and my thoughts than your thoughts.*
>
> *Isaiah 55:9 ESV*

To say that we don't need it or can operate without it is to say that God didn't know what he was doing when he created it. I refuse to let pride govern my interaction with the Spirit of God or his men and women. We need God's power to fulfill our calling.

The Scripture teaches that those who carry more spiritual virtue or power always impart to those who have less. The author of Hebrews writes:

> *It is beyond dispute that the inferior is blessed by the superior.*
> *Hebrews 7:7 ESV*

The New Living Translation of this verse says, "the person who has the power to give a blessing is greater than the one who is blessed."

You should connect with someone who has gone far beyond where you are and successfully accomplished what you want to do.

Because I understand and believe in impartation, I'm very guarded about who lays hands on me.

Years ago, I was holding a revival in New England in a rented church. Though the pastor who owned the building wasn't the host of the meeting, he attended the services every night.

At the end of the revival, being genuinely moved by

what God had done, that pastor met me in the parking lot as I was loading my truck.

"I'd like to lay hands on you and pray for you before you go, brother Ted," he said. I should note that the denomination that the pastor was a part of doesn't believe in the same things that I do as a Pentecostal. They would condemn certain full-gospel beliefs that the Scripture teaches.

"Why?" I asked him. He looked a little stunned. I don't think he knew what to say.

I don't want you to read this story and think that I'm arrogant. On the contrary, I want you to understand the importance of who lays hands on you. Not everyone is qualified to impart to you.

After a few seconds of silence, as he was trying to find the words to respond, I added, "There are only four reasons to lay hands on someone in the Bible—to baptize them in the Holy Spirit, to heal them, to bless them, or to appoint them to ministry."

He stared blankly at me, mulling over what I said.

"I'm already filled with the Spirit," I continued. "I'm not sick, I'm blessed, and I'm already in the ministry."

He laughed, realizing what I meant. I told him that I genuinely appreciated his heart and zeal and asked him if he would pray for me daily as I continued to work for the Lord. He said that he would be happy to do that.

Impartation for ministry and spiritual gifts is not something that should be done flippantly. It's a significant and important thing and should be treated as such. Paul directed Timothy to take caution when engaging in impartation:

> *Do not be hasty in the laying on of hands, nor take part in the sins of others; keep yourself pure.*
>
> **1 Timothy 5:22 ESV**

This was written so that Timothy wouldn't ordain and appoint people into ministry that weren't yet ready or worse—not even called.

As the writer of Hebrews teaches, the greater always imparts to the lesser. Impartation flows from the top down. The disciples never imparted to Christ; he imparted to them. It is always this way.

A SIGN OF HUNGER

Seeking impartation through the laying on of hands is another sign of spiritual hunger. Any time I've ever met a seasoned man of God who has made a significant impact, I ask them to lay hands on me. I pray that I'll never be too proud to do this.

It's important enough that I have traveled at my own expense, rented a hotel room and a car to attend a meeting where I could receive from a man of God. This isn't something I've done once or twice in my life; it's something that I do multiple times each year.

I want to encourage you to do the same. Actively seek impartation and take advantage of every opportunity to have hands laid upon you by the servants of God.

If you wanted to be a successful golfer, you wouldn't pay thousands of dollars each year to be trained by a hockey coach. It matters to whom you're connected.

Find someone who is doing what you're called to do and be humble enough to receive from them. God has a plan to take you further faster through the supernatural power of impartation, and the laying on of hands is one of the main avenues that will take you there.

PRINCIPLE 5

TAKE OWNERSHIP OF THEIR VISION

*Whoever believes in me will
also do the works that I do;
and greater works than these
will he do . . .*

—JOHN 14:12 ESV

IMPARTATION HAS NOTHING TO DO WITH COMPETITION AND EVERYTHING TO DO WITH COMPLETION. // #FURTHERFASTER

CHAPTER 10

In earlier chapters, I've mentioned the importance of serving the vision of the one from whom you want to receive a full impartation. It's vitally important to take ownership of their purpose and call and align yourself with it.

Every calling is set apart for a specific purpose. You can't attempt to "steal" an impartation and do what you want with it. The kingdom of God doesn't work that way. If that were your desire, you simply wouldn't receive an impartation.

Why? Because this would be evidence that you don't believe in the ministry of that individual and you'd be dishonoring them—two prerequisites we've already covered.

Notice that when Elisha succeeded Elijah, he didn't take Elijah's mantle to do something completely different than Elijah did. He stood in the prophetic office and continued to instruct the sons of the prophets as Elijah had done.

> *Elisha now returned to Gilgal, and there was a famine in the land. One day as the group of prophets was seated before him, he said to his servant, "Put a large pot on the fire, and make some stew for the rest of the group."*
>
> *2 Kings 4:38 NLT*

Elisha wasn't a rogue; he continued doing what Elijah was called to do.

The same is true of Joshua. God originally ordained Moses not only to deliver the Jews from slavery but to lead them into the Promised Land.

Because of Moses' sin, he was disqualified from completing his calling; however, through impartation, he transferred that task to Joshua.

Joshua didn't then take the Israelites in a different direction; he continued in Moses' calling and brought them into their promise. That's ownership of the vision.

Let's examine the ministry of Timothy for a moment.

> *So I urge you to imitate me. That's why*
> *I have sent Timothy, my beloved and*
> *faithful child in the Lord. He will remind*
> *you of how I follow Christ Jesus, just as*
> *I teach in all the churches wherever I go.*
> **1 Corinthians 4:16-17 NLT**

Even before the Apostle Paul died in Rome, Timothy was carrying out Paul's vision and giving his effort to help fulfill Paul's call. He was sold out to the spiritual father God had placed in his life.

IF YOU SEE ME WHEN I GO

When it was time for Elijah to be taken into Heaven and complete his ministry, Elisha asked for a double portion of his spirit. Although according to Elijah, he had asked a hard thing, he stated:

> *"...yet, if you see me as I am being taken*
> *from you, it shall be so for you, but if you*
> *do not see me, it shall not be so."*
> **2 Kings 2:10 ESV**

This is an interesting passage that we should take a moment to compare to a similar encounter. Elisha's double portion impartation was based upon whether or not he saw Elijah being taken.

The chariots and horsemen of fire were angelic and supernatural. Keep this point in mind.

Later in Elisha's ministry, the King of Syria wanted to kill him. When he found out Elisha was staying in Dothan, he surrounded the city with an army.

Gehazi, Elisha's servant, saw the Syrian army and became very afraid. "What are we going to do?" He asked.

"Do not be afraid, for those who are with us are more than those who are with them," Elisha replied.

What was he talking about? Gehazi didn't see anything but the enemy. To whom was Elisha referring? The answer required Elisha to pray. When he did, Gehazi's eyes changed.

> *Then Elisha prayed and said, "O Lord, please open his eyes that he may see." So the Lord opened the eyes of the young man, and he saw, and behold, the mountain was full of horses and chariots of fire all around Elisha.*
>
> *2 Kings 6:17 ESV*

Gehazi was not yet mature enough in the spirit to see into the prophetic realm. It required a prophetic prayer to open his eyes to the angelic forces surrounding their enemies. I've often said that he had "servant eyes" while Elisha had "prophetic eyes."

This was not the case for Elisha in 2 Kings chapter 2. After he and Elijah crossed the Jordan river and chariots appeared, no such prayer was necessary.

> *...Chariots of fire and horses of fire sepa-*
> *rated the two of them. And Elijah went*
> *up by a whirlwind into heaven. And*
> *Elisha saw it and he cried, "My father,*
> *my father! The chariots of Israel and its*
> *horsemen!" And he saw him no more.*
>
> **2 Kings 2:11-12 ESV**

Elisha was advanced and ready for promotion. He needed no assistance to see into the spirit realm. He could clearly see what God was doing.

Could it be that when Elijah said, "if you see me as I am being taken from you," it could have implied *If you see what I see* when I'm taken up from you?

I don't believe what he said to Elisha was merely a test to see if he would follow him until the end. He had already tested Elisha three times in that way.

Now, after all three transitions between their destinations, they had crossed the Jordan together. Elijah knew

Elisha wouldn't leave him. After all, he'd come all this way. Why leave now?

I believe his words were something deeper. If Elisha were genuinely ready to succeed Elijah, he'd be able to see what Elijah saw — and he did.

Notice that Elijah's mantle only fell to Elisha *after* he was taken up. Elisha was faithful, he could see, and he was ready.

WHAT DO YOU SEE?

My uncle, Pastor Terry Shuttlesworth, once preached this passage and used the phrase, "if we see eye to eye when I go."

Obviously, as Elijah's apprentice, Elisha had to see eye to eye with him. Part of impartation is being able to run with someone's vision. Whether it was Joshua, Elisha, the disciples, or Timothy, they all were able to advance their spiritual father's call and purpose.

The major challenge with a transfer of leadership is the transfer of vision. Instead of the next generation continuing in the purpose of the one before them, many try to alter the vision.

These transitions never seem to end well. Most of the time, it's because God never ordained that vision for the new direction in which it moves. The result? Failure.

Things fizzle out. God didn't ordain it, and so his resources are not committed to it.

> *Unless the Lord builds the house, those who build it labor in vain. Unless the Lord watches over the city, the watchman stays awake in vain.*
>
> *Psalm 127:1 ESV*

If God doesn't direct the vision, it will never prosper. This is why, in true impartation, a son takes ownership of the vision that God delivered to the father.

Throughout the Bible, there are examples of natural sons who disregarded their father's anointing and call.

Eli, who raised and trained the prophet Samuel, was a priest of God. While he spent time training Samuel and teaching him to hear the Spirit of God, his sons were not sensitive to the Spirit. How could Samuel turn out godly, and the sons be so evil?

> *Now the sons of Eli were worthless men. They did not know the Lord.*
>
> *1 Samuel 2:12 ESV*

The sad thing about this story is that Hophni and Phinehas were also priests unto God. They treated the offerings of God with contempt (1 Samuel 2:17).

One of the reasons they could not receive impartation is they refused to accept correction or direction because they would not listen to the voice of their father (1 Samuel 2:25).

As a result of their rebellion, God rejected Eli's household and removed his glory from them.

> *"Therefore, the Lord, the God of Israel, says: I promised that your branch of the tribe of Levi would always be my priests. But I will honor those who honor me, and I will despise those who think lightly of me.*
>
> ***1 Samuel 2:30 NLT***

What the Lord said here is such a vital principle to understand. I will *despise* those who think lightly of me. Thinking lightly of God's commands and directions is the equivalent of thinking lightly of God himself.

If Joshua had decided to take the Israelites somewhere other than Canaan after Moses' death, he would have been lightly esteeming the direction and purpose of God and, by extension, God himself.

We must remember that God's ways and thoughts are much higher than our ways and thoughts (Isaiah

55:8-9). The mistake that some people make is changing God's ways when they transition into leadership.

If God delivered a call and purpose to a particular vision, we cannot change it because we have an idea for a "better plan."

Real impartation is the power to accomplish what God has *already set in motion*.

ASK TO RECEIVE WHAT YOU WANT

. . . And Elisha said, "Please let there be a double portion of your spirit on me."

—2 KINGS 2:9 ESV

GOD DOESN'T HONOR VAGUE FAITH BECAUSE HE HAS PREPARED SPECIFIC BLESSINGS. // #FURTHERFASTER

CHAPTER 11

If you're married, have you ever had frustration arise in your relationship because you thought your husband or wife should have anticipated what you needed or wanted?

It could be something that deeply affected you, or it could be a very simple thing. After expressing your exasperation, your spouse looks at you and says something like, "How was I supposed to know you wanted me to do that? Am I a mind reader?"

No matter how long you've been married, I think you can identify with that kind of interaction.

Without a doubt, a lack of clear communication can be one of the most frustrating things in any relationship. Many feel isolated because of a breakdown in this area.

However, God *is* a mind reader. Literally. Of course, we use the more theological term: *omniscient*. Either way, God is aware of anything you could think or desire. If not, how could we have scriptures like this one:

> *Before they call I will answer; while they*
> *are yet speaking I will hear.*
> *Isaiah 65:24 ESV*

How can God begin to answer before you even call? How can he hear what you say before you finish speaking? It's because of his omniscience.

However, it's fascinating to me that although God knows our hearts, thoughts, and desires, he still requires us to make requests to him.

Why? Because the requests are a sign of faith. They show that we believe he can do what he said he would.

I would never ask a homeless person to buy me a home, nor would I ask my landscaper to perform brain surgery. Both for the same reason—I know they can't do it!

When we ask God, however, it's a sign that we have faith that he can and will do it.

That, by the way, is pleasing to God. The writer of Hebrews tells us that we can only please him by these actions of faith (Hebrews 11:6).

ANSWERS FOLLOW CALLS

How could you get angry at someone for not answering your phone calls if you've never called them? Sounds crazy, right?

But how many people get angry at God because he didn't just answer their prayers because he knows what they want?

I can't tell you how often I've heard things like, "Well, brother, God knows my need, and when he's ready, he'll bless me."

If that's how it worked, no one would ever have any needs because God is aware of all of them. God isn't moved by need; he's moved by faith. Notice what the prophet Jeremiah wrote:

> *Call to me and I will answer you, and will tell you great and hidden things that you have not known.*
>
> *Jeremiah 33:3 ESV*

This is how God moves. We call, he answers. It wasn't only this way in the Old Testament. When Jesus came, he upgraded our prayer status by giving us the power of using his name.

Now, in the New Testament period, we have a much

closer connection to Heaven because of our blood covenant with Jesus. Now, when we pray, we have a promise of God hearing us because of our relationship with Christ, Look at Jesus' words:

> *In that day you will ask nothing of me.*
> *Truly, truly, I say to you, whatever you*
> *ask of the Father in my name, he will*
> *give it to you. Until now you have asked*
> *nothing in my name. Ask, and you will*
> *receive, that your joy may be full.*
> *John 16:24 ESV*

We have an even greater authority in prayer in this New Testament covenant than anyone did in the Old Testament. As you see above, one of the reasons Jesus wants to answer your prayers is to fill you with overwhelming joy and strength.

SPECIFIC REQUESTS = SPECIFIC ANSWERS

Not only must we activate his presence by asking him in prayer, but we must also become extremely specific in *what* we ask him to do.

This key of making specific requests in prayer is so vital that entire books could be (and probably are) written on it.

Imagine arriving at a restaurant and being seated. You've had time to examine the menu, and your waiter returns to take your order.

"What can I get you for dinner?" He asks prepared to write your order on his notebook.

"I'd like to have a meal, please," you reply. The waiter peers over his notebook, quizzically at you.
"I'm sorry?" He says, thinking he misheard you.

"A meal," you say again. "I'd like a meal."

Although that may have made you smile as you read it, realizing how ridiculous of a conversation that would be, I'm sure you got my point.

> FAITH DOESN'T MAKE VAGUE REQUESTS BECAUSE GOD WANTS TO GIVE YOU SPECIFIC ANSWERS.

When you place an order, it's specific. Sometimes *very* specific. Have you ever gone to dinner with someone who couldn't just order a meal from the menu without seven substitutions or changes? I'm guilty of being that person from time to time.

"I'll have the cobb salad but with no avocado or blue cheese. Also, can you add extra chicken and bring the dressing on the side?" Does that sound familiar to you?

I'm sure you know people (not you, of course) who are quick to send their meal back if every stipulation wasn't met. The reason we get so specific is that we have particular desires. The reason someone may send their food back is that they have certain expectations.

That's how we need to be in prayer. If you're believing for an impartation, don't be satisfied with just anything. Press in and receive what you're expecting. Notice what the Apostle Paul wrote to the Philippian church:

> *Do not be anxious about anything, but in everything by prayer and supplication with thanksgiving let your requests be made known to God.*
>
> *Philippians 4:6 ESV*

When I was growing up in church, it was common for people to have "unspoken" prayer requests. This is when someone in church would submit a prayer request to the pastor or staff, but wouldn't tell you what it was.

Maybe it was a personal issue that they were embarrassed to admit or they were protecting the anonymity of a family member.

Whatever the case was, we would hear them recited along with the rest of the prayer requests during the service. The problem with an unspoken prayer request is that we can't know how to pray for it.

We must base our prayers upon God's Word for faith to be activated. If you're believing for deliverance, it does you no good for me to pray for healing.

Thus, the unspoken prayer request is ineffective. Paul made this point very clear in his letter to the Philippians. We have to make our requests *known*.

A DESK, A CHAIR, AND A BIKE

Dr. David Yonggi Cho is the pastor of the largest congregation in the world—Yoido Full Gospel Church in Seoul, Korea. Any church that boasts over one million congregants is a supernatural church.

In the early days of his ministry, however, Dr. Cho was not so successful. In fact, he was so poor that he didn't even have a desk upon which to study.

Not only did he not have a car, but he also didn't even have a bicycle on which to visit his members. All visitations were done on foot.

One day, he became so frustrated that he began to pray. I'm sure it sounded more like a complaint. He began to ask the Lord why he didn't have these things. Surely as a servant of God, he could have a desk, a chair, and a bike. So he prayed and asked the Lord.

Some time passed, and he still didn't have the desk, chair, or bike, so he asked the Lord why.

God spoke to him that, like many Christians, he hadn't been specific about what he wanted. Dr. Cho realized what the Lord was teaching him and quickly amended his list. He told the Lord that he wanted a desk made from Philippine mahogany, an American-made bicycle, and a chair with wheels on the bottom so he could "roll around his office like a big shot."

Not only did he make that specific request, but he also began to confess by faith that he already had those things.

A short time later, God answered his prayers as he was talking with a missionary. The missionary and his family had some things in a shipping crate that they wanted to give Dr. Cho.

When he went to look inside the crate, he found a desk made of Philippine mahogany, a slightly-used American-made bicycle, and a chair with wheels on the bottom so he could roll around like a big shot.[1]

I find it interesting that God didn't answer Dr. Cho's prayers until he became specific and made his requests known unto God.

How many times have we prayed generic and vague prayers with an "I'll take whatever comes" attitude?

It's time we made up our minds that we can and will have what God's Word promises and then take those promises with a bold faith that will not be denied.

The gospel of Matthew tells us that the violent take it by force (Matthew 11:12). Now is the time to engage with violent faith.

ELISHA GOT WHAT HE ASKED FOR

Let's take a closer look at the request Elisha made before Elijah was taken away from him. As they crossed over the Jordan river, Elijah wondered what he could do for Elisha. Let's examine the exchange.

> *When they had crossed, Elijah said to El-*
> *isha, "Ask what I shall do for you, before*
> *I am taken from you." And Elisha said,*
> *"Please let there be a double portion of*
> *your spirit on me."*
>
> *2 Kings 2:9 ESV*

This request is not only very specific, but it's also supernatural. How can anyone give double what they currently have? However, Elijah said God would grant it if Elisha were ready, as we covered in a previous chapter.

We also know that God literally fulfilled Elisha's request in that he produced thirty-two miracles by the end of his ministry. In contrast, Elijah had only produced sixteen.[2]

Elisha wasn't bashful about what he wanted. He had a desire to do great things for God, and he knew what he needed to accomplish his purpose.

You should never be timid about your desires, either. Your hunger should equip you with boldness to make a direct, specific request to the Lord. Remember, one of the side effects of insecurity or shame is timidity. Timidity will always keep you from stepping out in faith, let alone making specific requests.

> *Let us therefore come boldly to the throne*
> *of grace, that we may obtain mercy and*
> *find grace to help in time of need.*
> *Hebrews 4:16 NKJV*

Notice how God expects you to approach him — boldly to obtain mercy and grace. It's worth noting here that the word translated "grace" here is the Greek word *charis* that we discussed in chapter 3.

This was the word Paul used to refer to spiritual gifts when he was writing to the Romans and Corinthians. The boldness that Elisha had (that you must also have) is required to obtain these gifts.

The enemy would love it if he could deceive you into staying timid about what God has planned for you. He wants you to believe you're not worthy to receive the impartation that God has made available in your spiritual inheritance.

You must know that impartation is God's desire for you and that he has made you worthy to receive it.

POSITION DETERMINES PETITION

I want to make a very important point here. Elisha's *position* made room for his *petition*. This is the reason that all of the sons of the prophets were not able to obtain a double portion as he did.

It's also why I'm writing this chapter as step six in the process instead of step one or two. Not everyone is qualified to make specific requests.

Imagine how out of place it would have been for one of the sons of the prophets to have asked Elijah for a double portion of his spirit.

He had never served him, traveled with him, taken on his personal vision, or make decisions that proved he believed in the ministry of Elijah.

Clearly, he would not be qualified to make a request of that nature. Elisha, on the other hand, was the *only* one qualified. God operates by this principle. He qualifies the one who is calling on him by their commitment. Look what Peter wrote:

> *For the eyes of the Lord are on the righ-*
> *teous, and his ears are open to their*
> *prayer. But the face of the Lord is against*
> *those who do evil.*
>
> 1 Peter 3:12 ESV

Notice that the position of righteousness is what qualifies you for answered prayer. David knew the opposite was also true:

> *If I had cherished iniquity in my heart,*
> *the Lord would not have listened.*
>
> Psalm 66:18 ESV

David is saying that if he had been out of position, it would void his petition.

This is why you can't pick and choose how you'll receive impartation. There is an order to God's process. Imagine how foolish you'd feel trying to climb a ladder by starting on the eleventh rung. You always start at the bottom to climb to the top.

Now that you're in the position to make that request make sure you ask not only boldly but specifically.

What are you believing God will do? What do you want to take place in your life? Make a decision that you will not only stay in a position of boldness, but you will cry out from your heart exactly what you want to have happen in your life.

God has a plan to use you in a mighty way. He's waiting for you to make your request known.

PRINCIPLE 7

STAY CONNECTED FOR A CONTINUAL FLOW

But he gives more grace.
Therefore it says, "God op-
poses the proud but gives
grace to the humble."

—JAMES 4:6 ESV

IMPARTATION, LIKE A LADDER, DOESNT JUST TAKE YOU TO THE NEXT LEVEL, IT KEEPS YOU THERE. // #FURTHERFASTER

CHAPTER 12

I can remember walking out of my house in Virginia, looking up toward the gutters, and letting out a heavy sigh at least once a year.

Pine trees surround our house. For that reason (and because I was too lazy to install gutter guards), my gutters would get filled to overflowing with pine needles.

I only tried cleaning them out once. Just once. It required a thirty-foot ladder, and I don't do well with heights.

I got to the top rung and started pulling clumps of needles and gunk out of the gutter and dropping them to a pile on the ground below.

I was a bit free with my movement at the top of the ladder until I felt it shift, and my footing became less secure. I'm not saying a spirit of fear gripped me or that I prayed in "speed tongues," but let's just say I came down to terra firma for a break.

It was at that moment I realized that you don't just need a ladder to go up; you need a ladder to *stay up*.

Imagine how angry you'd be if someone were holding a ladder that size for you, and when you got to the top, they tried to yank it out from under you.

I'm sure you'd start shouting at them to replace it. You'd think they were insane if they said, "You were already at the top. I didn't think you needed it anymore."

Of course, you need it.

That's the point of this section. You don't just need a connection to impartation to go higher; you need one to stay at that place.

CRAM SESSION CULTURE

If you've ever studied for a test, you may have used the cram session method. The night before the test, you repeatedly review and maybe even have someone quiz you until the early hours of the morning as you try to retain as much knowledge as you can.

Often, the reason students do this is because they care more about the result of a test than actually retaining the knowledge of the subject.

It's not that great of a long-term study method. In fact, some researchers suggest that we only remember about twenty percent of quickly-learned material after thirty days.[1]

Aren't you glad a surgeon doesn't have to cram before each surgery? Those who value the information they're studying stay connected to it faithfully throughout their entire lives.

However, few people want to dedicate themselves to any kind of life-long pursuit. We expect everything to be quickly accessible in today's society. We have fast-food restaurants and overnight shipping.

For many, this kind of thinking has bled over into spiritual things. Some only want to be quickly anointed to be seen by others. This spiritual pride is an element that will make God your opponent.

> *But he gives more grace. Therefore it says, "God opposes the proud but gives grace to the humble."*
>
> *James 4:6 ESV*

As I covered in a previous chapter, this element of spiritual pride was the issue that Simon the Sorcerer struggled with in Acts chapter 8.

He was used to amazing the people of Samaria with

his manifestations of magic. Even after his conversion, he didn't entirely conquer that area of his life. When he saw the new believers being filled with the Spirit as Peter and John laid hands on them, he desired that power quickly. He offered to buy it.

We know his desire was carnal rather than holy because the apostles rebuked him for it. Had he only stayed faithful to their teaching and become more mature, he'd have realized that every believer has that power already.

It's this desire to be seen that pushes some people into this spiritual "cram-session culture." They want quick promotion for self-promotion. They only stay connected long enough to get a leg up. However, humility and a genuine desire to serve will keep us connected long term.

CONNECTED UNTIL THE END

I've always found Elisha's unwillingness to disconnect from his mentor interesting. Although Elisha was called by God to be Elijah's replacement, what he received from Elijah was conditional.

Elijah tested him three times in transition from city to city on his final journey. Each time, Elisha replied, "As the Lord lives, and as you yourself live, I will not leave you." (See 2 Kings 2:2, 4, 6)

What if Elisha hadn't stayed connected to Elijah? What if he thought he'd gone far enough? He would have missed Elijah's transition into Heaven and, thus, missed receiving his mantle. When you disconnect, you miss out on the continual flow. It's important never to feel like you've "made it" and no longer need the help of others.

At the very least, you'll need the prayers of your brothers and sisters in Christ. Notice what Paul wrote to the church in Ephesus (one of the last letters of his ministry).

> *And also [pray] for me, that words may be given to me in opening my mouth boldly to proclaim the mystery of the gospel, for which I am an ambassador in chains, that I may declare it boldly, as I ought to speak.*
>
> *Ephesians 6:19-20 ESV*

Notice that Paul didn't have a spirit of pride. He could have said, "I'm your apostle. I don't need your help or your prayers; you need mine."

However, even toward the end of his ministry, Paul knew he needed others in the body of Christ. Humility is the key to increase in the kingdom of God.

We need to not only seek out impartation, but we also need to stay connected to those with whom God has attached us.

If you're a minister, there should always be times throughout the year that you pause the work of the ministry to receive ministry yourself. Every believer should do the same. Impartation is not only a source of promotion, but it's also a source of encouragement and strength.

Notice that Paul told the Roman church that the impartation he would deliver to them would cause them to be established (Romans 1:11). He was describing the divine strength that would come upon the work they were doing for the Lord.

The same is true for you. When you stay connected to continual impartation, you're receiving continual strength to accomplish your particular purpose for God.

IMPARTATION BRINGS ENCOURAGEMENT

Without a doubt, one of the most wonderful benefits of continual impartation is spiritual and natural encouragement and refreshing.

This is such a needed element throughout your Christian life and service and cannot be underestimated.

Christian leaders need encouragement more than ever before.

A 2017 Barna report showed that 47% of pastors are less satisfied with their current church and ministry, and many are at risk of burning out.[2] The enemy will do whatever he can to convince you to quit.

That's why the Word of God encourages us never to grow tired of doing what we're called to do.

> *And let us not grow weary of doing good,*
> *for in due season we will reap, if we do*
> *not give up.*
> *Galatians 6:9 ESV*

One of the ways we can avoid burnout is a steady flow of encouragement through impartation.

When King Saul was troubled by an evil spirit, David, who was mightily anointed by God, came and released divine power through praise. It refreshed King Saul immediately. (See 1 Samuel 16:23.)

Never forget that someone else's anointing and power can bring immediate strength and refreshing to your life and ministry.

Often, the enemy will make a strong effort to force you to quit right before you persevere into the breakthrough that you're expecting.

FURTHER FASTER

The sad truth is that many have quit before seeing the promise of God fulfilled in their lives. Make up your mind that you'll never be that person.

DON'T QUIT TOO SOON!

You never know how close you are to the next level. Never quit.

In his famous book *Think and Grow Rich*, Napoleon Hill tells a story entitled *The Man Who Quit Too Soon*. The legend goes as follows:

> An uncle of R. U. Darby was caught by the "gold fever" in the gold-rush days, and went west to dig and grow rich. He had never heard that more gold has been mined from the thoughts of men than has ever been taken from the earth. He staked a claim and went to work with pick and shovel.
>
> After weeks of labor, he was rewarded by the discovery of the shining ore. He needed machinery to bring the ore to the surface. Quietly, he covered up the mine, retraced his footsteps to his home in Williamsburg, Maryland, and told his relatives and a few neighbors of the 'strike.' They got together money for the needed machinery

170

and had it shipped. The uncle and Darby went back to work the mine.

The first car of ore was mined and shipped to a smelter. The returns proved they had one of the richest mines in Colorado! A few more cars of that ore would clear the debts. Then would come the big killing in profits.

Down went the drills! Up went the hopes of Darby and Uncle! Then something happened. The vein of gold ore disappeared! They had come to the end of the rainbow, and the pot of gold was no longer there. They drilled on, desperately trying to pick up the vein again—all to no avail.

Finally, they decided to quit.

They sold the machinery to a junk man for a few hundred dollars, and took the train back home. The junk man called in a mining engineer to look at the mine and do a little calculating. The engineer advised that the project had failed because the owners were not familiar with 'fault lines.' His calculations showed that the vein would be found just three feet from where the Darbys had stopped drilling! That is exactly where it was found! The junk man took millions of dollars in ore from the mine because he knew enough to seek expert counsel before giving up.[3]

Imagine how many blessings and victories never took place because someone was tricked into giving up too soon.

Recently, Bishop Rick Thomas, who pastors Abundant Life—the church we attend, was teaching about this very thought.

He reinforced his teaching with this illustration: when you drive past a cemetery, what you don't realize is that the graves aren't just filled with the bodies of those who once lived, but books that were never written, businesses that were never started, and ministries that were never launched.

Why? Because they either quit too soon or they never started in the first place.

The continual flow of impartation is a safeguard against burnout and discouragement. Paul, writing to the Romans, said it this way:

> *That is, that we may be mutually strengthened and encouraged and comforted by each other's faith, both yours and mine.*
>
> *Romans 1:12 AMP*

Like the seven sons of Sceva in Acts chapter 19, many are trying to claim an authority they've never been attached to or received from. There's no strength in that.

As my father has taught for many years, if you want to have a gift, you've got to sit under a gift. This is because the greater always imparts to the lesser, never the other way around.

> *Yet it is beyond all contradiction that it*
> *is the lesser person who is blessed by the*
> *greater one.*
>
> *Hebrews 7:7 AMP*

We've got to make up our minds that pride will never keep us from seeking and staying connected to impartation from those who are operating at a higher level of blessing and manifestation than we are.

STAY HUMBLE. STAY HUNGRY.

If you claim no one fills that role for your life, you're probably lying to yourself.

One of the greatest acts of humility I've ever seen was when the late Evangelist Oral Roberts asked a young Dr. Rodney Howard-Browne to lay hands on him at Rhema Bible Church in Tulsa, Oklahoma in 1993.

Dr. Roberts—who was seventy-five years old at the time—had laid hands on over one million people and seen countless salvations, signs, wonders, and miracles. He was one of the most prolific men of God in the history of America (and probably the world).

In December of 1989, Dr. Rodney and Adonica Howard-Browne emigrated to the United States from South Africa and settled in Kentucky. They then began holding revival meetings.

MEEKNESS IS THE SUPERNATURAL KEY TO GOD'S GREATNESS.

In 1993, revival broke out in Lakeland, Florida, and manifestations of the joy of the Lord filled Carpenter's Home Church and then spread to many others.[4] God was using Drs. Rodney and Adonica mightily at a very young age.

Later that year, Dr. Rodney was holding revival services at Rhema Bible Church in Tulsa, Oklahoma. One night as he was ministering, he saw Dr. Oral Roberts in the crowd, acknowledged him, and asked him to come forward.

The power of God began to flow, and the joy of the Lord filled the auditorium, and many began laughing in the spirit.

As the Spirit of God was touching his people, Dr. Roberts said to Dr. Rodney, "The Lord wants you to say something to me . . . because there's one more thing I have to do before my angel comes for me."[5]

Dr. Rodney proceeded to prophesy to Dr. Roberts who received the word by faith. One of the things prophesied was that God would renew Dr. Roberts' youth. He went on to live for sixteen more years before going home to be with the Lord at the age of ninety-one.

It still amazes me that a man of God who had been shaking the world for decades was humble enough to lift his hands and receive a word of prophecy from an evangelist in his early thirties who was just beginning his ministry.

Obviously, as we've learned, this would be the exception to the rule, but God ordained this moment. We can learn a lot from Dr. Roberts' humility. Jesus taught:

> *"Blessed are the meek, for they shall inherit the earth.*
>
> *Matthew 5:5 ESV*

Truly, meekness is the supernatural key to inheritance. I shared that story with you because no matter how old you are or how long you've been serving the Lord, there is someone who is currently more fruitful than you are. Don't allow pride to destroy you.

If the enemy cannot stop you from working, he will attempt to overwork you. Rest and refreshing are necessary elements in maintaining a fruitful life and accomplishing your purpose for the Lord.

Jesus made a point to drill this lesson into his disciples when they returned to him with their ministry testimonies. Rather than focusing on their completed work, he led them away.

> *The apostles returned to Jesus and told*
> *him all that they had done and taught.*
> *And he said to them, "Come away by*
> *yourselves to a desolate place and rest*
> *a while." For many were coming and go-*
> *ing, and they had no leisure even to eat.*
> *Mark 6:30-31 ESV*

This passage tells us that they were so busy with the work of the Lord that they hadn't even eaten. Obviously, in context, this means they hadn't eaten any food.

However, can I suggest to you that a parallel spiritual principle also exists? At some point, you must eat spiritually as well.

> *Your words were found, and I ate them,*
> *and your words became to me a joy and*
> *the delight of my heart . . .*
> *Jeremiah 15:16 ESV*

One of the ways impartation will come is in the form of the Word of God ministered to you. As the Word comes to you, it will establish and strengthen you. Ezekiel, the prophet, experienced this principle at the time of his divine calling as the Word of God set him upon his feet. (See Ezekiel 2:2.)

Similarly, as Paul ministered to the Ephesian elders in Acts chapter 20, he explains what the power of God's Word can accomplish in a person's life.

> *And now I commend you to God and to the word of his grace, which is able to build you up and to give you the inheritance among all those who are sanctified.*
>
> *Acts 20:32 ESV*

The Word can build you up and give you an inheritance. The Greek word translated "build you up" in English means to erect a structure. Impartation is God's way to build in and around you, what he has called you to accomplish for him.

Knowing this fact, the devil wants to separate you from God's "workshop." He never wants to see you increase and expand. Pride is the trick that keeps you from being built.

No matter how old you get or how much God promotes you, continue to pursue impartation. Make time for spiritual encounters in the midst of your work for the Lord. Never take for granted those with whom God has connected you. Value them. Bless them. Attach yourself to their purpose and call. God will bless you for it.

CHAPTER 13

GIANTS FOR DINNER

Do not fear the people of the land, for they are bread
for us. Their protection is removed from them . . .
— Numbers 14:9 ESV

Imagine that you were taking a missionary trip to a third-world nation to help a group of impoverished people. Each night, you would be ministering to one thousand hungry souls.

Before you leave on your journey, a wealthy man contacts you and tells you that he would like to write you a check so that you can give $50,000 to each of the families in the village. What a gift!

When you arrive in the village and begin to distribute the financial aid to the families, do you think they care how old you are?

Absolutely not. As I wrote previously, age is not the determining factor in your ability to make a spiritual impact in the world. On the contrary, the resources you carry determine the impact you can make. Because of your connection with that wealthy man, he was able to impart resources and gifts to you. That connection gave you the ability to help others regardless of your age.

He imparted resources to you that he labored a lifetime to build. Notice that although he was the one who worked to amass great wealth and financial influence, impartation allowed your mission to instantly benefit from his years of labor.

You didn't have to work for thirty years to gather the necessary wealth to bless the natives of that village. You were able to do so because someone else had developed the resources and then delivered them to you.

Similarly, in the body of Christ, we are all supposed to benefit from and build upon the gifts, revelation, wisdom, and work of the previous generation.

They have spent time building spiritual strength (which we are also required to do), yet we don't have to begin where they began. Because of impartation, we get to start building where they finished building.

YOU ARE WHAT YOU EAT

After Moses brought the Israelites out of Egypt and through the Red Sea, they wandered through the wilderness on their way to the Promised Land.

Finally, they progressed to the place where they could send spies into Canaan to see what the Promised Land was like.

One man from each of the twelve tribes of Israel was chosen to join a scouting party sent on a reconnaissance mission to gather intel on God's promise.

When they returned to give a full report to Moses and the assembly, the opinion (and more importantly, the perception) of the group was divided. Ten of the men were filled with fear, and two were filled with faith.

When speaking on this subject at churches, I'll ask the congregation the names of the two men who had faith. "Caleb and Joshua," they always shout in reply.

Then, for effect, I'll ask anyone who can to name any of the other ten spies. No one ever can. This example allows me to drive home the point, *faith makes you famous, but fear makes you forgettable.* Ten of the men agreed that the Promised Land was beautiful. However, they said:

> *But the people living there are powerful .*
> *. . We even saw giants there, the descendants of Anak!*
>
> *Numbers 13:28 NLT*

This lack of faith was extremely frustrating to Joshua and Caleb because they had faith in God's promise. Caleb immediately spoke up in protest and said, "Let's go at once to take the land. We can certainly conquer it!"

The rest of the spies vehemently disagreed with him and began to list the reasons why it wouldn't work. They began to spread the propaganda that their enemies were too strong and too big. They even painted a visual picture for Israel by saying, "Next to them we felt like grasshoppers!" (See Numbers 13:30-33.)

This negative report was so disturbing to Joshua and Caleb that they tore their clothes to show their distress and began to plead with the nation of Israel:

> *Do not rebel against the Lord. And do*
> *not fear the people of the land, for THEY*
> *ARE BREAD FOR US. Their protection*
> *is removed from them, and the Lord is*
> *with us; do not fear them.*
> *Numbers 14:9 ESV (Emphasis added)*

They are bread for us. That phrase is so important. Joshua and Caleb understood that they would devour their enemies.

Keep in mind throughout this section that the battles you fight and win are not arbitrary. Each one has a purpose that is linked to the success of your future. The strength to increase and accomplish your purpose at the next level is dependent upon the battles you fight and win. The Apostle Peter wrote:

> *Be sober, be vigilant; because your adver-*
> *sary the devil walks about like a roaring*
> *lion, seeking whom he may devour.*
>   *1 Peter 5:8 NKJV*

Notice that you can either devour your enemies, or you can be devoured. The level of spiritual strength you have determines the battles you can win.

Solomon shows us this truth in the form of a proverb when he wrote: "If you faint in the day of adversity your strength is small" (Proverbs 24:10).

Just as Old Testament saints weren't all operating at the same level of power, spiritual strength isn't automatically delivered to you because you're a Christian.

> *Finally, be strong in the Lord and in the*
> *Strength of his might.*
>   *Ephesians 6:10 ESV*

Paul wrote this to what was arguably the most spiritually mature church in the New Testament—the Ephesians. He commanded them to be strong. That lets us know it was possible for the believers—Spirit filled or not—to be weak. One of the ways you can build strength is by continuing to win battles by your faith. The more enemies you defeat, the more strength you will have.

Because of his love for you, God will never allow you to face enemies that you can't conquer. No situation is impossible for you.

> *God is faithful, and he will not let you be tempted beyond your ability, but with the temptation he will also provide the way of escape . . .*
> *1 Corinthians 10:13 ESV*

Previous battles that are won on previous levels of your purpose give you strength and prepare you for more significant battles at higher levels of your purpose.

David understood this before he ever became the King of Israel. At one time, he looked like a nobody. He was stuck in a field tending sheep.

His brothers were warriors. His father didn't even believe in him. So much so, that when Samuel came to his house to anoint the next king, Jesse—David's father—presented his other seven sons to the prophet and left David in the field. *David couldn't be a king,* he obviously thought to himself.

It looked like David was nothing and had no purpose.

However, there came a time that a lion and a bear broke into the sheepfold, and David was required to win those battles. After looking at the many victories David won throughout his life, these two against mere animals may seem surprisingly unimpressive. After all, a mountain lion is nothing compared to a battle-hardened giant.

But don't forget that David was still at his lowest level and fighting lower-level battles, which were giving him strength for the future.

Before David attempted to fight Goliath, King Saul questioned him because of his age and size. David proceeded to give the king a lesson in the progression of his spiritual strength.

> *Your servant has struck down both lions and bears, and this uncircumcised Philistine shall be like one of them . . .*
> *1 Samuel 17:36 ESV*

It's important to note that David pointed to his previous victories as proof that he would devour Goliath in the same way.

But how could he be sure that he was at a giant-devouring level and not still stuck in lion and bear mode?

Impartation.

After David had killed the lion and bear, Samuel,

the prophet, came to find him. God instructed Samuel to impart a new level of anointing and power to David to prepare him for the next level of his purpose. So the prophet Samuel brought his flask of anointing oil to Jesse's house and anointed David in front of his brothers. The Bible reveals why David could be so sure he was ready to devour a giant:

> *So as David stood there among his brothers, Samuel took the flask of olive oil he had brought and anointed David with the oil. And the Spirit of the Lord came powerfully upon David from that day on . . .*
>
> *1 Samuel 16:13 NLT*

David was standing at a new level of strength and power because of the impartation he received from Samuel. He'd already tasted lion and bear jerky; now it was time to try giant steak.

A REMINDER OF YOUR ENEMIES
FOR THE REMAINDER OF YOUR ENEMIES

This wasn't the last time God used David's previous battles as fuel to give him future victory. Seven years after David had devoured Goliath, King Saul was pursuing him angrily.

God had already rejected Saul and selected David to be the next king. Saul was trying to locate David to kill and remove him.

Jonathan, Saul's son, and David's best friend, discovered that his father truly wanted David dead. As Jonathan and David previously agreed, Jonathan warned him when he found out the truth about the king's plans.

David escaped to the town of Nob to see a priest named Ahimelech. When he arrived at the temple, he asked the priest, "Do you have a spear or sword? The king's business was so urgent that I didn't even have time to grab a weapon!"

Ahimelech's response is a compelling picture of how God uses your testimonies — previous victories you've won by faith — to position you for your next triumph:

> *"I only have the sword of Goliath the Philistine, whom you killed in the Valley of Elah," the priest replied . . . "Take that if you want it, for there is nothing else here."*
>
> *"There is nothing like it!" David replied "Give it to me!"*
>
> **1 Samuel 21:9 NLT**

God purposely brought David to the one place that held a reminder of his precious victories — victories that seemed impossible.

It was God effectively saying, "If I could do *that* back then, I can do *this* now."

Think about how David must have felt as he held Goliath's sword in his hand once again. Imagine the surge of strength that flooded his body as the events of that battle replayed like a film in his mind.

David wasn't allowed to touch King Saul, so the sword served no purpose in battle. It was merely a token that would transport him back to the right frame of mind for what was to come.

The reminder of his victory against Goliath wasn't God's attempt to make David live in the past. On the contrary, God wasn't done working with and using David. It was a flash briefing of the strength that was still available to David. The power still linked to his purpose. This is a lesson for us. It's very important *how* you view your testimonies.

REMEMBER THE PAST. NOW FORGET IT.

The truth is, it takes maturity and development to use what God did in your past properly. The dangerous thing about looking backward is that you can become stuck in the past. That's extremely hazardous because it hinders you from moving forward into the more significant things God has planned for your life.

Assuming you moved away from where you grew up, have you ever traveled back home during a holiday or for an event and reconnected with some of the people from your high school? (God help you if it was a high school reunion.)

Why is there inevitably that guy who still wears his varsity jacket, class ring, and hasn't changed his hairstyle since his senior year? He loves to talk about the "good old days" when life was so much more simple.

> THE PAST IS ONLY A PICTURE THAT WILL HELP YOU PAINT YOUR FUTURE.

Obviously, I'm overemphasizing a stereotype to make this point, but on some level, it rings true for you. Why are people like Mr. High School working dead-end jobs they hate, waiting for the weekend, and unable to progress in life?

You've got to let go of the past to step into the future. I'm not devaluing the wonderful things that happened in the past. I can be nostalgic. But, the things God has accomplished in your past are building blocks for a greater future.

God, himself, wants you to remember the past . . . and then forget it.

Speaking through the prophet Isaiah, God began to encourage his people by telling them that although they had seen him do incredible things, the best was yet to come. After spending time itemizing the things he'd done for them, he said:

> *But forget all that—it is nothing compared to what I am going to do.*
> *Isaiah 43:18 NLT*

God then revealed that he had already begun to do something new, and their responsibility was to catch the vision of what it was. (See Isaiah 43:19.)

Without a doubt, God's people could have stayed connected with the miracles of the past, but that would have ensured those were the only miracles they would've received. By obeying God's command to forget the things of the past and focus on the future, they were headed for even greater days.

TRADITION CANCELS GOD'S TRANSACTION

It's easy to become locked into what God *has* done. If we're not careful, we can turn what God did in the past into tradition—but that would cancel God's transaction.

Once God commands something new, he's done

with the old. When he created a new covenant with us through the blood of Jesus Christ, who was sacrificed as the Eternal Lamb, he was finished with the old covenant that was enacted by the sacrifices of spotless bulls, goats, and lambs. We have a new covenant established upon better promises (Hebrews 8:6).

Although God's nature doesn't change, his methods of manifesting his nature can change. The previous example is an excellent picture of this. God has always (and will always) require blood sacrifices for sin. In the Old Testament, they gave an annual sin offering to cover their sins for that year.

Now that Christ has died, his blood is a continual, ever-present sacrifice for the sins of man. (See Hebrews 10:8-12.) God's nature didn't change; his methods did.

If we tried to keep the old covenant functional by making animal sacrifices instead of accepting Christ's sacrifice, we would miss out on the new thing God was doing and cancel his transaction in our lives.

There's an interesting story in the book of Ezra. The people of God began to rebuild the temple. This second temple replaced Solomon's Temple, which was destroyed years before when Jerusalem was conquered, and many were taken into Babylonian exile.

When the foundation of the new temple was laid, a very odd thing took place. The way God's people responded to the new foundation is a picture of the dangers of holding on to the past after God begins to move into the future. Remember, God said that what he had done in the past was nothing compared to what he was about to do.

Look what happened among the people once the foundation had been laid:

> *But many of the older priests, Levites, and other leaders who had seen the first Temple wept aloud when they saw the new Temple's foundation. The others, however, were shouting for joy. The joyful shouting and weeping mingled together ring a loud noise that could be heard far in the distance.*
>
> *Ezra 3:12-13 NLT*

Was the previous temple magnificent? Absolutely! But it didn't exist anymore except in their memories. A new temple was being built for the almighty God again. No one had a right to mourn.

The wonderful things God has done in your past are not there so you can travel back and attach yourself to the past. They are fuel for your future. They are reminders of how powerful your God is.

David repeatedly discovered this truth throughout his life. He was able to devour lions and bears, which put him in position to devour a giant. The strength of that victory launched him into defeating nations.

It was out of previous life experience that David was able to write verses like these:

> *You prepare a table before me in the presence of my enemies; you anoint my head with oil; my cup runs over.*
>
> **Psalm 23:5 NKJV**

As you continue to win battles by faith, God is preparing you for promotion to your next level. If you're faithful over little, God will make you ruler over much. (See Matthew 25:23.)

If God couldn't trust David to protect his father's sheep from lions and bears, how could he trust him to defend his nation from giants and evil men?

Never be discouraged about the level on which you're currently living. Become excited to devour the enemy God has placed in front of you, knowing that your victory is the only fuel that will take you higher.

MANIFESTATIONS WITHOUT LOVE ARE LIKE
VACATIONS WITHOUT A HEARTBEAT.
MEANINGLESS. // #FURTHERFASTER

CHAPTER 14

THE LAUNCHPAD OF LOVE

And if I have prophetic powers, and understand all
mysteries . . . but have not love, I am nothing.
1 Corinthians 13:2 ESV

Reverend Asa Alonso Allen, known throughout his ministry as A.A. Allen, was a Pentecostal evangelist during the Voice of Healing movement. He held massive tent crusades throughout the United States and saw many mighty healing miracles.

Brother Allen was a man who had the heart of God and, through supernatural compassion, sought to see people saved and healed. Sometimes he would fast and pray throughout the entirety of his twenty-one-day tent crusades believing God for miracles to take place.

In fact, many miracles did take place. One of my favorite miracles of his ministry took place under the tent. When I was young, my father had many of Brother Allen's crusades on video, and I remember watching them.

One of my favorite videos was entitled "The Monkey Boy." (A portion of this video is available to view on our website at www.miracleword.com/monkeyboy)

As Brother Allen holds the young boy and sets him on the pulpit, he shows the crowd that the legs have no bones by twisting them in every direction.

The boy, who feels Brother Allen's supernatural love, lays his head on Allen's shoulder.

"Yes, honey?" Brother Allen responds. "Poor little thing," Brother Allen says as he hugs the boy and begins to weep. "Oh, God!" He cries. "In the name of Jesus, make him whole! Let him walk!"

Moments later, after prayer and the laying on of hands, Brother Allen sets the boy down on the platform, and he begins to stand and take steps! This unusual and creative miracle displays the supernatural power of Christ that's still at work today.

As you watch the video, you can see the mighty compassion that emanates from Brother Allen. This is a personality trait of Jesus Christ. This love and compassion is the launchpad for the power of God to move.

> *When he went ashore he saw a great*
> *crowd, and he had compassion on them*
> *and healed their sick.*
>
> *Matthew 14:14 ESV*

In a time when Christ wanted to be alone after the death of John the Baptist, crowds continued to follow him. Notice that he didn't send them away. Divine compassion came upon him, and he ministered to them.

Love is the catalyst for the manifestations of Christ. After the Apostle Paul gives in-depth teaching of the gifts of the Spirit in 1 Corinthians chapter 12, he finishes that section of writing by saying:

> *But earnestly desire the higher gifts. And I will show you a still more excellent way.*
>
> *1 Corinthians 12:31 ESV*

Of course, Paul didn't break his letters down into chapters. At the time of writing, it was one solid letter. He uses this transitional sentence to move into teaching about love.

He taught the Corinthians, who had an abundance of the gifts of the Spirit in operation in their church, that without love at the center, none of those gifts matter. (See 1 Corinthians 13:1-3.)

I pray that this final chapter of the book leaves an imprint of purpose upon your mind and your spirit. We don't receive impartation to bolster our ego or social standing within the church body. Its purpose is to give us the supernatural abilities needed to minister to those whom God loves. Like Christ, we should strive to have strong compassion for the men and women around us, whether they are sinners or saints.

It's important to remember that *nobody* was a Christian during the time of Christ's ministry — he had not yet died. He loved and ministered to sinners. When asked why he spent time around such unclean people, he answered:

> *"Those who are well have no need of a physician, but those who are sick. I came not to call the righteous, but sinners."*
> **Mark 2:17 ESV**

One of the main reasons we must keep love at the forefront of our lives and ministries is because it's the fuel that allows your faith to function. Notice that Paul told the Galatian church that faith works through love (Galatians 5:6).

This is because God is love. You can't remain outside of God and think your faith for miracles is going to function.

You can't hate or discriminate against someone because of their skin color or economic status and expect God to use you.

Notice that John wrote and gave us this exact teaching in his first epistle:

> *If anyone says, "I love God," and hates his brother, he is a liar; for he who does not love his brother whom he has seen cannot love God whom he has not seen.*
> *1 John 4:20 ESV*

You also can't hold grudges and be unforgiving and expect your faith to work. When Christ taught his disciples about the power of faith to move mountains in Mark chapter 11, he didn't conclude the teaching without making sure they understood the attitude they should have when petitioning God for miracles:

> *And whenever you stand praying, forgive, if you have anything against anyone, so that your Father also who is in heaven may forgive you your trespasses."*
> *Mark 11:25 ESV*

I've noticed that the mightiest men and women of God have always been the ones who walked in love toward God's people. Dr. T.L. Osborn, known by some as the Apostle of Love, held mass crusades in over seventy nations and saw millions saved and healed by purely preaching what he called "the message that works." He was preaching the love of God.

His revelation of God's great love and power are visible in books he released like *God's Love Plan.* He understood that a loving God wouldn't want to leave people helpless under the power of sin and death. God wants to restore the dignity of humanity.

Other great men of God had the same revelation. I remember hearing Bishop David Oyedepo, pastor of one of the world's largest churches, pray saying, "Lord, if you will not bless my people, do not bless me."

He didn't have an "every man for himself" mentality. He had a love for God's people that wanted to see them abundantly blessed.

SUPERNATURALLY EMPOWERED & SUPERNATURALLY EMPLOYED

I dealt with the danger of pride in a previous chapter. However, as it is a sin that God hates and an enemy of your impartation, I want to mention it again briefly.

Paul introduced himself in multiple letters as a *slave* of Christ. In modern translations, it may be rendered as a *bondservant* or a *servant* of Christ.

The reason for the different translations is because

the word translated slave (as in Romans 1:1) is the Greek word *doulos*. Because of cultural differences, this term needs a bit of explaining.

Slavery has an understandably negative connotation in our society because we immediately think of American slavery, which was ultimately abolished by the results of the Civil War.

However, the word *doulos* (or *ebed* in the Old Testament) doesn't necessarily mean the same thing as the definition of slavery we're used to hearing. A more accurate translation of this word is bondservant.

Many times, a bondservant was someone who was working to pay off their debts by serving as a worker for the one whom they owed. After the debt was paid or the contract expired, they were free again.

However, provision was made for certain servants who decided that they wanted to stay with the family they had been serving. This was the procedure:

> *But if he says to you, 'I will not go out from you,' because he loves you and your household, since he is well-off with you, then you shall take an awl, and put it through his ear into the door, and he shall be your slave forever.*
>
> *Deuteronomy 15:16-17 ESV*

It's interesting to me that John the Beloved, Jesus' apostle, who wrote the book of Revelation, referred to himself as the Lord's bondservant (Revelation 1:1).

John was the man who *laid his head* on the chest of Jesus at the Last Supper. Jesus declared that he alone was the Door (John 10:9).

What an incredible New Testament picture of this Old Testament procedure. John, the disciple whom Jesus loved, would have literally laid his ear on the Door of Christ, knowing that he was his bondservant forever.

Later, when receiving the book of Revelation from Christ, he wrote:

> *He who has an ear, let him hear what the*
> *Spirit says to the churches . . .*
> *Revelation 2:7 ESV*

Obviously, he's not talking only to those who are born with natural ears, instead, to the ones who have their ears open in the Spirit. He tells us in Revelation 1:1 that God gave him this revelation to show his bondservants — those whose ears are connected to the Door, which is Christ.

Paul identified himself as one of these bondservants. This signifies that he isn't in control of his own life or destiny; he has turned it over to the Lordship of Jesus

Christ. He disciplined his natural desires on a daily basis so that he would better serve the Lord. (See 1 Corinthians 9:27.)

This is such an important point as we conclude the teaching on impartation. We don't receive impartation to become great in the eyes of men or for our selfish purposes. We are empowered to be servants of God.

There will always be a daily battle against the desires of the flesh. It's a constant war.

> *Walk by the Spirit, and you will not gratify the desires of the flesh. For the desires of the flesh are against the Spirit, and the desires of the Spirit are against the flesh, for these are opposed to each other, to keep you from doing the things you want to do.*
>
> *Galatians 5:16-17 ESV*

Pride is a function of the flesh. It brings destruction and causes you to fall. As you receive impartation, never forget that it's God Spirit using you and not your natural gifts or abilities.

I once heard Pastor Enoch Adeboye tell a story about this principle. One night, he was walking through the Redeemed Christian Church of God compound in Nigeria, praying and believing God for greater things. God used him to expand the RCCG from approximately 150 churches in Nigeria to churches in many nations of the world. The Lord stopped him as he was praying.

"Bend down and draw a man in the dirt," the Lord said. Pastor Adeboye obeyed. "Now, take your foot and wipe the man away." Pastor Adeboye did it until all that was left were streaks from his shoe in the ground.

"If you ever forget who is responsible for your success and victory, I will wipe you from the earth, and no one will remember your name," the Lord said.

That may seem like a heavy warning, but when your ministry is expanding around the world, and millions of people gather to hear you speak, humility is more necessary than ever.

Although we are children of God, we must remember we are his servants. May the words of John the Baptist be burned into your spirit as you work for the Lord:

"He must increase, but I must decrease."
John 3:30 ESV

I pray that the compassion of Christ overtakes your heart as you receive more and more impartation. I pray that this book has given you hunger to constantly seek impartation and increase in your work for the Lord.

May love always be the launchpad of your ministry. As you walk in divine love and hunger for the things of God, I pray that your family, life, and ministry increase beyond anything you could have imagined.

There is no limit to what God can use you to accomplish for his kingdom. Never-ending increase will be your story. I leave you with a powerful proverb that will fill you with expectation. I love you.

> *But the path of the righteous is like the light of dawn, That shines brighter and brighter until the full day.*
>
> *Proverbs 4:18 NASB*

ACKNOWLEDGMENTS

I'm always thankful to the the Lord for the spirit of wisdom and revelation. The more I study the Word of God, the more I realize you can never exhaust its expansive truth and wisdom.

I want to thank all those who made this book possible by lending me their help and time during the project. I'd especially like to recognize:

Carolyn. You believe that I can do anything and always encourage me to press forward in excellence. I love you. I'm proud of you.

Madelyn, Brooklyn, and Teddy III. This book is truly for you. By faith, you will surpass anything that your mother and I have done for the Lord. Never stop pushing.

Dad and Mom. You raised me in a home where the power of impartation was always apparent. Thank you for showing me the way.

Pastor Terry Shuttlesworth. Your teaching and preaching on covenant and impartation have been invaluable and opened my eyes to the power of God. Thank you.

Tiffany Jane Penelope Gertrude Farley. Thank you very much for the hours you spent helping me proofread, copyedit, and check for errors. I'm buying you a crate of the world's finest tea.

Stephanie Iaquinto. Thanks for letting me blow up your phone with questions about style and form.

Miracle Word Partners. Thank you for being excited about this project. I appreciate everyone who preordered this book. I apologize for the delay. I believe it was worth the wait.

NOTES

CHAPTER 3

1. Imparting of Spiritual Gifts. The Assemblies of God, 2015, ag.org/Beliefs/Topics-Index/Gifts-Imparting-of-Spiritual-Gifts. (NOTE: Since the time of publication, the denomination has removed this position paper from their website.)
2. Potts, John. "The Roots of Charisma." SpringerLink, Palgrave Macmillan, London, 1 Jan. 1970, link.springer.com/chapter/10.1057%2F9780230244832_2.
3. Ibid.
4. Oyedepo, David. *Exploits in Ministry.* Ota: Dominion House, 2010. 209. Print.

CHAPTER 5

1. "The Royal Bastards of Medieval England." The Royal Bastards of Medieval England, by Chris Given-Wilson and Alice Curteis, Barnes & Noble, 1995, pp. 48–52.
2. Pollard, A. (1901). "Beaufort, John, first Earl of Somerset and Marquis of Dorset and of Somerset (1373?–1410)" . In Lee, Sidney (ed.). Dictionary of National Biography (1st supplement). 1. London: Smith, Elder & Co.

CHAPTER 7

1. "Founders Online: From George Washington to John Trumbull, 25 June 1799." National Archives and Records Administration, National Archives and Records Administration, founders.

   archives.gov/documents/Washington/06-04-02-0120.

CHAPTER 8

1. Sumrall, Lester. Pioneers of Faith. Harrison House, 1995.
2. Montgomery, Mel. "Howard Carter's Story." Rediscovering Pentecost, 2007, web.archive.org/web/20081006074950/http://brothermel.com/howardcarterariseyoungman.aspx.

3. ibid.
4. Malcomson, Keith. Pentecostal Pioneers Remembered: British and Irish Pioneers of Pentecost. Xulon Press, 2008.
5. Parr, John Nelson. Incredible. Published by the Author, Fleetwood, Lancs., England, 1972.
6. Sumrall, Lester F. Adventuring With Christ. LeSEA Publishing Company, 1988.
7. ibid.
8. Lake, John G. Spiritual Hunger. Christ for the Nations, 1979.

CHAPTER 11

1. Cho, David Yonggi. The Fourth Dimension. Bridge-Logos Publishers, 1979.
2. For a full list of Elijah and Elisha's miracles, see Finis J. Dake's Notes on "Miracles of Elijah and Elisha" after the note on 2 Kings 2:10.

CHAPTER 12

1. Metos, Thomas H. The Human Mind: How We Think and Learn. Franklin Watts, 1990.
2. The State of Pastors: How Today's Faith Leaders Are Navigating Life and Leadership in an Age of Complexity. Barna Research Group, 2017.
3. Hill, Napoleon. Think and Grow Rich: The Complete Classic Text. Jeremy P. Tarcher/Penguin, 2008.
4. Pinsky, Mark I. "When Holy Laughter Starts, Some Find It Hard To Stop." OrlandoSentinel.com, 4 Oct. 2018, www.orlandosentinel.com/news/os-xpm-1996-09-01-9608310934-story.html.
5. Video can be found at https://www.youtube.com/watch?v=HiaxTIRPUp8

ABOUT THE AUTHOR

Evangelist Ted Shuttlesworth Jr. has been preaching the gospel for close to two decades. Ted has been privileged to minister across the United States, as well as in other nations, with many creative miracles reported.

Ted is an author, weekly podcast host, and the founder of Miracle Word University—an online training resource designed to raise a new generation of leaders and equip believers for their God-given purpose.

He is a graduate of Rhema Bible College and currently resides in Florida with his wife, Carolyn, and their three children, Madelyn, Brooklyn, and Teddy III.

PRAYER OF SALVATION

Heavenly Father,

Thank you for sending your Son, Jesus, to die for me. I believe that You raised him from the dead and that he is coming back soon.

I'm asking you to forgive me of my sin and make me brand new. Give me holy desires to pray and read your Word. Empower me by Your Holy Spirit to live for You for the rest of my life.

You are the Lord of my life. I thank you that the old life is gone and a new life has begun, in Jesus Name, Amen.

....

If you prayed this prayer, please contact us. We would like to send you a free gift, pray for you and help you take your next steps in Christ.

info@miracleword.com

GET STARTED WITH ANY
BIBLE COURSE FOR **ONLY $69!**

Finally, affordable online Bible training courses that will build your faith as well as your knowledge of God's Word and equip you for your calling.

We'll cover subjects like Divine Healing, Pneumatology - the Person and Baptism of the Holy Spirit, Answered Prayer - Understanding how prayer works & how to receive answers, Mountain-Moving Faith & Worship Keyboard

MIRACLEWORDU.COM

When the children of Israel went into captivity, they hung their harps on the trees and began to weep. They locked their praise away. The very thing that had brought them victory so many times in the past had been kicked to the curb.

The enemy knows how powerful your praise is. That's why he uses a spirit of heaviness to steal it from you. Praise is the pathway into every blessing God has prepared for you. From healing to prosperity and everything in between, praise is God's prescription for victory. This new book will show you how to unlock the covenant blessings of Heaven through the supernatural power of praise.

SHOP.MIRACLEWORD.COM

OR ON YOUR PREFERRED E-READER

DIVINE PROTECTION BELONGS TO YOU BECAUSE OF YOUR COVENANT WITH GOD

It seems fear has intensified in America and around the world. Whether it's viral outbreaks of disease, the economic downturn of 2008, breaking news about groups like al-Qaeda, Boko Haram, and ISIS, school shootings, natural disasters that seem to be escalating around the world, or attacks like we saw in Paris and Brussels, the hearts of people seem to be filled with terror.

Should Christians be worried as the days grow darker before the coming of the lord? IS there hope and portection for God's people? I believe there is. This book will reveal how you can access the protective power of God Almighty, while the workbook will take you into a deeper study of your biblical covenent.

SHOP.MIRACLEWORD.COM
OR ON YOUR PREFERRED E-READER

YOU MAY OWN THE FASTEST CAR IN THE WORLD BUT IF THE GAS TANK IS EMPTY IT'S NOT GOING ANYWHERE.

That's why the overwhelming joy of the Holy Spirit is so vital to your Christian life. The Bible tells us that the joy of the Lord is our strength. If the enemy is able to steal your joy, he has also stolen your strength and the momentum to do what you've been called to do. The Apostle Paul told the church that God's kingdom is made up of three elements: righteousness, peace, and joy in the Holy Spirit. Surprisingly, many Christians today are satisfied to only have one of the three kingdom components present in their lives! This book will show you that there are clear paths that lead to living a life of overwhelming joy. Don't allow the enemy to steal your peace and joy ever again. You can shed the skin of depression and enter into feather-light living for Jesus Christ beginning today!

SHOP.MIRACLEWORD.COM
OR ON YOUR PREFERRED E-READER

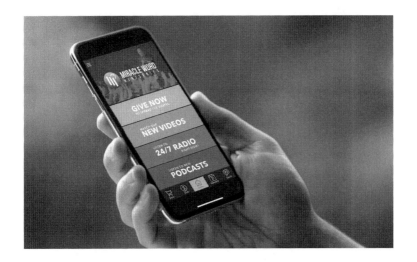

DOWNLOAD OUR FREE APP

you can hear preaching 24/7, watch our youtube
videos, listen to our weekly podcasts and much more

FOLLOW US ON SOCIAL

(f) **/MIRACLEWORDMINISTRIES**

(y) **@TSHUTTLESWORTH**

(◉) **@TEDSHUTTLESWORTH**

(▶) **TED SHUTTLESWORTH JR.**